SUPERVISION OF PS
AND COUNSELLING

SUPERVISION OF PSYCHOTHERAPY AND COUNSELLING

Making a place to think

Edited by
Geraldine Shipton

OPEN UNIVERSITY PRESS
Buckingham · Philadelphia

Open University Press
Celtic Court
22 Ballmoor
Buckingham
MK18 1XW

email: enquiries@openup.co.uk
world wide web: http://www.openup.co.uk

and
325 Chestnut Street
Philadelphia, PA 19106, USA

First Published 1997
Reprinted 2000

Copyright © The Editor and Contributors 1997

All rights reserved. Except for the quotation of short passages for the purpose of criticism and review, no part of this publication may be reproduced, stored in a retrieval system, or transmitted, in any form or by any means, electronic, mechanical, photocopying, recording or otherwise, without the prior written permission of the publisher or a licence from the Copyright Licensing Agency Limited. Details of such licences (for reprographic reproduction) may be obtained from the Copyright Licensing Agency Ltd of 90 Tottenham Court Road, London, W1P 9HE.

A catalogue record of this book is available from the British Library

ISBN 0 335 195121 (pb) 0 335 19513 X (hb)

Library of Congress Cataloging-in-Publication Data
Supervision of psychotherapy and counselling / edited by Geraldine
  Shipton.
    p. cm.
  Includes bibliographical references and index.
  ISBN 0-335-19513-X. — ISBN 0-335-19512-1 (pbk.)
  1. Psychotherapists—Supervision of. 2. Counselors—Supervision
of. I. Shipton, Geraldine.
RC459.S875 1997
616.89'14—dc20   96-33218
                                                                              CIP

Typeset by Type Study, Scarborough
Printed in Great Britain by St Edmundsbury Press Ltd, Bury St Edmunds, Suffolk

This book is dedicated to the memory of Dr Jim Gomersall, who died during the writing of it, completing corrections to his chapter the day before his death

CONTENTS

Notes on contributors ix
Acknowledgements xi

1 Introduction 1
   Geraldine Shipton

Part 1 Knowing about supervision

2 Supervision today: the psychoanalytic legacy 11
   David Edwards
3 Supervision as a space for thinking 24
   Phil Mollon
4 Shame, knowledge and modes of enquiry in supervision 35
   Alan Lidmila
5 How the patient informs the process of supervision: 47
   the patient as catalyst
   Jonathan Bradley

Part 2 Art, technology and fantasy in supervision

6 Fantasy, play and the image in supervision 61
   David Maclagan
7 The image's supervision 71
   John Henzell
8 The use of audiotapes in supervision of psychotherapy 80
   Mark Aveline
9 Interpersonal process recall in supervision 93
   Peter Clarke

Part 3 Developing the quality of supervision

10	Peer group supervision *Jim Gomersall*	107
11	The triangle with curved sides: sensitivity to issues of race and culture in supervision *Colin Lago and Joyce Thompson*	119
12	Becoming a supervisor *Deborah Pickvance*	131
13	The place of supervision *Geraldine Shipton*	143

Index 151

NOTES ON CONTRIBUTORS

Mark Aveline is a consultant psychotherapist, Nottingham Psychotherapy Unit, chair of training committee, South Trent Training in Dynamic Psychotherapy, and President, British Association for Counselling. His publications include *Group Psychotherapy in Britain* (1988), *From Medicine to Psychotherapy* (1992) and *Research Foundations for Psychotherapy Practice* (1995).

Jonathan Bradley is a consultant child psychotherapist and senior tutor at the Tavistock Clinic and Head of Child Psychotherapy Services, City and East London Health Authority.

Peter Clarke is a chartered clinical psychologist, psychotherapist, trainer and former senior lecturer in clinical psychology at the University of Sheffield.

David Edwards is an art therapist, psychotherapist and lecturer in art therapy at the Centre for Psychotherapeutic Studies, University of Sheffield.

Jim Gomersall was formerly senior lecturer in psychotherapy, former director of the Postgraduate Diploma in Psychotherapy, University of Sheffield and former honorary consultant psychiatrist, Sheffield Health Authority.

John Henzell is an artist, art therapist and lecturer in art and psychotherapy, Centre for Psychotherapeutic Studies, University of Sheffield.

Colin Lago is a counsellor and trainer and director of the University Counselling Service, Sheffield. His publications include *Race, Culture and Counselling* (1996) and he has written and published training videos including *Issues of Race and Culture in Counselling Settings* (1989, with Joyce Thompson).

Alan Lidmila is an analytic psychotherapist and supervisor in private practice and lecturer in psychoanalytic psychotherapy at the Centre for Psychotherapeutic Studies, University of Sheffield and associate of the Westminster Pastoral Foundation, Leeds.

David Maclagan is a writer, artist and art therapist. He is also lecturer in art and psychotherapy at the Centre for Psychotherapeutic Studies, University of Sheffield. His publications include *Creation Myths* (1977).

Phil Mollon is a psychoanalytic psychotherapist, clinical psychologist and clinical manager with North Hertfordshire Health Trust. His publications include *The Fragile Self* (1993) and *Multiple Selves, Multiple Voices: Working With Trauma, Violation and Dissociation* (1996).

Deborah Pickvance is a psychotherapist in general practice and with Sheffield Women's Counselling and Therapy Service, and supervisor in private practice.

Geraldine Shipton is a psychotherapist and supervisor in private practice and lecturer in psychotherapeutic and psychoanalytic studies in the Centre for Psychotherapeutic Studies, University of Sheffield.

Joyce Thompson is a counsellor, supervisor and trainer who has researched race in counselling supervision. She is a former psychiatric nurse and senior education manager in the NHS. She has worked on the training video *Issues of Race and Culture in Counselling Settings* (1989, with Colin Lago).

ACKNOWLEDGEMENTS

I would like to acknowledge David Edwards, who co-organized the conferences which gave rise to most of the chapters in this book; all the participants, speakers and workshop leaders who took part in them; and Colin Brady, who introduced me to the quotation from William James which appears in Chapter 13.

1

INTRODUCTION

Geraldine Shipton

Supervision is an odd word suggesting both exceptional clear-sightedness and a superior vantage point from which to look, as if the supervisor has only to cast his or her eyes over the work in question for the key elements to appear. Whilst this may be a true description of some supervisory consultations, most consultants feel this is frequently not the case and that, even when it is, the task of the supervisor is to help the supervisee gain access to a more advantageous position from which to consider their work. The place for thinking about psychotherapy is continuously constructed by the supervisor, often on the basis of his or her past experience of being supervised, through the creation of an optimal setting and attitude for both parties. This book introduces the reader to several different ways of thinking about supervision which should take most readers, if not beyond their own habitual viewpoint, then at least to less familiar perspectives.

The increasing professionalization and standardization of psychotherapy and counselling in Britain have given rise to the publication of many new books which are concerned with aspects of practice, including some very influential books on supervision (two of note are Hawkins and Shohet 1989; Langs 1994). Welcome as such books have been to a range of practitioners in the helping professions, they do not set out to engage with the psychotherapeutic practices which this book tackles, such as the therapeutic relation to the image or to imagination, for example, or to consider the nature and effect of knowledge in supervision or the impact of particular technologies. A space is thereby vacant for these and other questions which concern the contributors to this book.

Special mention should be made of Hawkins and Shohet's book as it was the first significant attempt in Britain to set out firm foundations for supervision which were usable by professionals from different helping disciplines. The authors erected a systematic model for supervisors (the process model) which encompassed excellent ideas from analytic and humanistic practice in psychotherapy. The writers also had an eye to the wider social and institutional matrix within which supervision takes place. The present book does not deal with such issues and is geared solely to psychotherapy (albeit of various kinds), therapeutic counselling, and training in these professions. The 'how to do it' nature of Hawkins and Shohet's book is one of its major strengths and one of its weaknesses too. It dwells on 'reality' factors to a greater degree than opted for by some of the writers in this book, although we have tried to avoid simplistic divisions between reality and fantasy. Bollas and Sundelson (1995: 66) describe the 'freedom of expression' of psychoanalytic work where, for example, 'silences are complex inner experiences that call into being and consciousness fragments of thought and feeling that move more like the structure of musical thought than cognition proper'. It is in the spirit of understanding this kind of thinking that some of the chapters are written, even where the writers themselves are not psychoanalytically oriented. Some contributors have paid attention to the more concrete aspects of the supervisory relationship with a view to making available for thought the unconscious or pre-conscious factors which may be affecting the supervisee and the supervisor. A range of approaches and theoretical allegiances is represented in the book.

Unlike Langs (1994) this book does not propose one particular method for supervision: instead, the reader is invited to step outside of his or her usual way of thinking about supervision of clinical work and to entertain a few novel ideas about the theory or practice of it. Some chapters will clearly represent familiar territory for certain readers but we hope others will stimulate fresh ideas or enthusiasms.

The book grew out of a wish to understand the therapeutic milieu in which the editor and several of the contributors to this book started their professional careers. This attempt to locate the 'Sheffield' model of supervision (which has now become almost defunct) within the broader history of psychoanalysis and psychodynamic psychotherapy led to two conferences on supervision, and to the eventual publication of some of the talks and workshop material that has been developed since those conferences.

The 'Sheffield' model of supervision entailed exploration of the psychotherapist's own reactions to patient or client material. The focus on countertransference meant that, at times, supervision was nearly indistinguishable from psychotherapy. In a situation of limited availability of fully-trained analysts or psychotherapists, such an approach, no doubt, brought a level of expertise to a geographic region which supported little analytic 'culture'. However, for trainee psychotherapists the solution to a practical problem produced a far more difficult professional and psychodynamic problem about boundaries and ethical conduct. The outcome, after a series of difficult discussions, was the establishment of a split between supervision and psychotherapy for all trainee psychotherapists on the Sheffield course – a solution which brought Sheffield in line with other analytically-oriented training courses in Britain. It seems clear that some positive aspects of the 'Sheffield' model, such as its emphasis on the countertransference, may be retained in supervision, provided that the patient or client is not obscured in the process and that the supervisee is able to occupy a self-reflective position without ultimate loss of professional role or boundary. However, trainees are usually not as able to plumb the depths of their own countertransference feelings as are those who have already completed a successful analysis or psychotherapy and may need more privacy for self-reflection.

Another pertinent issue is that supervisors of trainees need to adopt a more evaluative role than do supervisors of qualified psychotherapists. Thomas Ogden (1995) suggests that supervisees need to feel relaxed with both their supervisor and with themselves if they are to make analytic use of their own reactions. He proposes that the most mundane of thoughts which pass through the therapist's mind during a session with a patient can provide clues to the inter-subjective relationship which is unfolding. However, being able to pay attention to such rêveries is, he points out, a considerable achievement:

> As with most aspects of analytic technique, attention to and use of the analyst's private discourse that is seemingly unrelated to the patient runs counter to the character defences that we have developed in the course of our lives. To attempt to loosen our dependence on these character defences often feels like 'tearing off a layer of skin', leaving us with a diminished stimulus barrier with which to protect the boundary between inner and outer, between receptivity and over stimulation, between sanity and insanity.
>
> (Ogden 1995: 702)

Clearly, such a shift in attitude requires considerable confidence in oneself and in the supervisor.

Contents

David Edwards, who organized the conferences with the editor (and who was a keen instigator in getting this book into print), writes about the tradition of supervision and the bifurcation of that tradition whose roots go back to Vienna and Budapest. There is no consensus amongst the writers about which traditions they espouse, but as the chapters progress, it will become clear that some new ideas about supervision are being fashioned, and that many perspectives may inform not only our appreciation of clinical supervision, but also our awareness and knowledge about how people learn from their own and others' experience. Indeed, there is a theme which runs through all the chapters which is about curiosity and its careful management, as a helpful impulse or a potentially intrusive or seductive one.

The first section of the book ('Knowing about supervision') opens with four quite distinct but related chapters which tackle the differing traditions of experiential and didactic models of learning and their specific gravity within each writer's perception of how best to understand supervision. Some distinctions are made between training supervisions and the supervisions of professionals who are already qualified, be it as psychotherapists, counsellors, art therapists, or others responsible for clinical work of a therapeutic kind. This said, however, it would be wrong to suggest there are always clear distinctions between supervisees who are trainees or who are trained. It may be the case that it is much easier to learn and develop once the pressure to demonstrate capability and competence is reduced. In this respect, supervision is an aspect of professional development which involves a permanent commitment to learning and training. The extensive literature on supervision which David Edwards has surveyed is evidence that supervision is currently a focus of increasing theoretical and practical interest in many disciplines.

Phil Mollon suggests that supervision is a space for thinking about emotional material and that it has to be protected from being turned into an opportunity for evacuation ('dumping') or non-thinking. He describes the different mental processes that are involved in the creation of new insights and how the supervisor can foster supervisees' capacity to think freely about their work. This chapter introduces a key theme in the book, which is that psychotherapy and supervision are creative processes, not simply the reproduction of a set of learned skills. No 'wild' supervision is being suggested here, but more a mindfulness about how to keep in step with the workings of the unconscious without losing touch with reason and ethics.

Many other themes outlined in the first section are picked up and applied to practice in later chapters. For example, there is concern in the first section over how the supervisor thinks about his or her own role and manner of thinking, speaking and behaving. Alan Lidmila discusses several notions of enquiry which may prompt a supervisor's questions and which may incur shame in the supervisee rather than the capacity to think. The relationship between asking questions, respect for the supervisee, and therapeutic detachment is also central to Peter Clarke's chapter, which focuses on using a mode of enquiry imported from the United States called Interpersonal Process Recall.[1]

The positioning of the supervisor's self in the relationship between the patient and the therapist is an issue for many of the chapters. Jonathan Bradley draws a distinction between knowing from personal experience rather than from a more formal acquaintance, and explains how unconscious factors determine what can be known. He examines how the supervisor might struggle with processes which obscure or clarify the supervisor's or the therapist's view of the patient and considers what is catalytic in an encounter, be it therapeutic or supervisory. David Maclagan's chapter in Part Two opens up the same problematic to the freedom which fantasy bestows. In this chapter, he encourages us to appreciate the benefits of what he terms a 'distance to the literal' in supervision. The whole of the second section ('Art, technology and fantasy in supervision') allows four very different perspectives to be represented on the use of visual and audio material in supervision.

John Henzell asks us to respect and learn from the role of the image in the supervision of image-making therapies. Imagination is a vital factor which makes itself felt both at the theoretical and practical level throughout the book. Sometimes this is an enabling potential, as demonstrated by John Henzell, but it can also be disabling when unconscious phantasy is of a persecutory nature.[2] Mark Aveline confronts the fears and anxieties which can affect supervision where taped sessions are used and, refusing an easy divide between fantasy and reality, suggests direct and subtle means of working with these problems. Interestingly, this reiterates the other concern of the first section, which is about power and its 'safe practice' in supervision. Both Mark Aveline and Peter Clarke, in different ways, examine the empowering potential of using audio or video equipment within well thought-out and clearly defined parameters.

The final section of the book ('Developing the quality of supervision') is an attempt to apply imagination and sensitivity to some frequently met issues in the world of psychotherapy and counselling. The problems of providing a supervisory function for groups of workers whose managers may not be keen to support the individual supervision of their clinical work is discussed by Jim Gomersall. His many years of experience in using psychodynamic principles to help illuminate the work of colleagues in the National Health Service involved a great deal of peer supervision. In a therapeutic culture which has not been well endowed with financial resources or well-established psychoanalytic institutes, he helped to promote a psychodynamic psychotherapy which practitioners from other traditions could learn from and to which they could also contribute.

The racial and cultural implications which can often be overlooked in supervision and which are closely tied up with power and authority are examined by Colin Lago and Joyce Thompson. Writing from their own experience as trainers and supervisors of person-centred counsellors, and drawing on Joyce Thompson's research into cross-cultural supervision, they highlight the complicated nature of the presentation of the self in cross-cultural counselling and therapy.

The penultimate chapter in this section unites the good sense of many of the others in preparing the new supervisor for a task which one hopes will be rewarding as well as challenging. Deborah Pickvance takes a balanced look at what the prospective supervisor needs to have thought about before he or she embarks on the supervision of others.

In the concluding chapter, the place of supervision is revisited and loosely summed up and some suggestions made about future lines of thought which it may be fruitful to pursue.

Who are the supervisees?

Not everyone who does psychotherapeutic work is designated a psychotherapist or counsellor by profession. Art therapists, occupational therapists, nurses, doctors, psychologists and social workers may be trained as psychotherapists or not, but they are often engaged in therapeutic work which requires supervision. It can be hard to find supervisors who really understand the special skills and needs of colleagues whose setting or practice belongs to a discipline which differs from their own. Unfortunately, there are simply not enough well-qualified supervisors outside the metropolis who are available to supervise colleagues from their own profession. The results can be unsatisfactory, refreshing, calamitous or illuminating. It is hoped that this book sheds some light on possible problems of cross-profession and cross-orientation supervision and may even suggest some profitable solutions.

Some psychotherapists and counsellors are unperturbed by the notion of eclecticism in their work, despite the tendency nowadays towards increased consistency and congruence between theoretical affiliation and practice, especially as regards accreditation (this is leaving aside models of therapy and counselling whose expressed underpinning is a well-thought-out integrative model). Personally, I do not find eclecticism appealing either practically or theoretically, and do not supervise others whose clinical values differ dramatically from my own. However, not everyone is convinced that eclecticism is a problem, provided concepts can be integrated rather than mixed up, as Jim Gomersall and Deborah Pickvance demonstrate in their chapters. Furthermore, some people do not enjoy the freedom to choose from amongst a variety of colleagues for help with their work. Such people may well enjoy not only reading about how others theorize and practice supervision, but may also want to incorporate alternative ideas into their own work. More probably, supervisors will wish to reframe certain innovative ways of thinking or practising from within their own orientation, setting or personal style. An awareness of difference, or disagreement even, can help to clarify and validate one's own practices as well as introduce an opportunity for learning how to do or conceptualize something differently.

Where colleagues are involved with training others, it seems particularly useful to find out about how helpful concepts can be applied to such areas. The question of whether or not a good psychotherapist or counsellor can be trained or whether they are simply improved by training remains undecided. Since there has been an upsurge in the number of qualifying courses for psychotherapists and counsellors towards the end of this century, this issue is an important one. Whatever one thinks about training, most practitioners would agree that the supervisor plays a crucial role in professional development. Indeed, an understanding of particularly difficult times in psychotherapy supervision may elucidate the process of both teaching and learning psychotherapy (Allphin 1987), rather as research findings on the 'working alliance' in psychotherapy have illuminated critical aspects of the therapeutic process (Horvath and Greenberg 1994). It is also clear that where supervision is carried out in an unethical way that the 'apprenticeship' of the supervisee can be to a malignant set of norms which can lead to the abuse of patients and clients (Jehu 1994).

All the chapters emphasize the complexity of supervision, and share a common desire to enhance the understanding of how to be a good supervisor and to encourage others to feel confident about an activity which many find extremely rewarding. In explaining why he writes about psychoanalysis, André Green (1972: 3) has said that he does so as a testimony to what he has learned and in order to maintain a self-image which he can recognize, as well as to seize 'the elements of a complex experience, often obscure and sometimes elusive, to organize it into a coherent vision which ensures that it does not completely escape our understanding'. Something of this wish to capture, and to share with others, a moment of 'truth' and understanding is one of the reasons that colleagues choose to supervise others. In writing about their thoughts on supervision in this book, I think that there is the same wish to synthesize and share thought and experience by all the contributors.

Notes

1 Interpersonal Process Recall tends to use the term 'inquiry', which suggests a formal, organized mode of questioning rather than the term 'enquiry'; accordingly, the IPR convention is followed when IPR is being discussed. Elsewhere the term 'enquiry' is employed.
2 Fantasy and phantasy are spelled differently in accord with psychoanalytic convention when a distinction is made between a conscious imaginative process (fantasy) and an unconscious one (phantasy).

References

Allphin, C. (1987) Perplexing or distressing episodes in supervision. How they can help in the teaching and learning of psychotherapy. *Clinical Social Work Journal*, 15(3): 236–45.
Bollas, C. and Sundelson, D. (1995) *The New Informants: Betrayal of confidentiality in psychoanalysis and psychotherapy*. London: Karnac Books.
Green, A. (1972) *On Private Madness*. Madison, CT: International Universities Press, Inc.
Hawkins, P. and Shohet, R. (1989) *Supervision in the Helping Professions*. Milton Keynes: Open University Press.
Horvath, A.O. and Greenberg, G.S. (eds) (1994) *The Working Alliance: Theory, practice and research*. New York: John Wiley and Sons, Inc.
Jehu, D. (ed.) (1994) *Patients as Victims: Sexual abuse in psychotherapy and counselling*. Chichester: John Wiley and Sons.
Langs, R. (1994) *Doing Supervision and Being Supervised*. London: Karnac Books.
Ogden, T.H. (1995) Analysing forms of aliveness and deadness of the transference–countertransference. *International Journal of Psycho-Analysis*, 76: 695–709.

PART 1

KNOWING ABOUT SUPERVISION

This first part of the book starts with the historical origins of the tradition of supervision and goes on, through four different chapters, to consider the nature of knowing or thinking in supervision.

2

SUPERVISION TODAY: THE PSYCHOANALYTIC LEGACY

David Edwards

Introduction

The contemporary literature on clinical supervision is now as varied as it is specialized. This literature, emanating from a wide range of professional disciplines, theoretical and personal perspectives, is also one which continues to expand at a frenetic pace.[1] Thus far, however, very little has been written specifically on the history of supervision. Valuable though much of the wisdom and experience contained within the vast literature on supervision undoubtedly is, the majority of books and articles tend to be concerned with recent and particular aspects of the exposition or application of a specific model. Few of these texts seek to provide a historical overview of the subject, Marshall's article on the history of supervision within psychoanalysis being a notable exception to this general rule (Marshall 1993). In view of the importance now attached to supervision across the whole range of helping professions this omission is a significant one, especially as the way supervision is approached and organized today either incorporates, or stands in opposition to, theories concerning the nature of psychotherapeutic relationships pioneered by Freud and his followers at the turn of the century.

This chapter has, therefore, two main aims. First, to trace the origins of supervision, a line of enquiry which inevitably leads back to the birth of psychoanalysis, and second to evaluate the impact that disagreements within psychoanalysis, at the very beginning of organized training, appear to have had upon its subsequent development. Disagreements that, in essence, concern the issue of whether, or to what extent, supervision ought to be concerned with helping the therapist or trainee learn about their own feelings as opposed to learning about therapeutic techniques and strategies. In addressing these issues my aim is not to catalogue the history and development of each and every mode of supervision currently available, examples of which may be found elsewhere in this book. Though possibly illuminating, such an ambitious project is beyond the scope of this chapter. My intention, rather, is to examine the particular influence psychoanalysis has exerted upon the ways in which supervision is currently practised and to discuss some of the problems and difficulties that arise from this.

An examination of the ideas and concepts that have influenced and informed the development of supervision would seem to be both timely and relevant. Not least because one of the most notable features of supervision evident in the literature is that each school or model of supervision, having developed its own rationale and protocols, often appears to function with only a very limited appreciation of the history and theoretical foundations of alternative, possibly competing, paradigms. Two problems may be identified as arising from this lack. First, that 'this is how I supervise' might be interpreted as meaning 'this is the correct and only way to supervise'; a point of view it would be difficult to provide convincing evidence to support (Holloway 1984). And second, that what might be said to be of value in the supervision process may be diminished or overlooked in favour of promoting a particular model of practice irrespective of the therapist's or trainee's level of training, needs, preferences or theoretical orientation. Either approach to supervision, if applied inflexibly, is likely to limit the potential helpfulness of supervision. This issue would seem to be particularly important in the area of training where trainees are typically exposed to a variety of experiences and theories concerning the psychotherapeutic process. While some schools of psychotherapy insist that trainees are supervised by a more experienced clinician working within a clearly defined theoretical framework, as, for instance, is the case for analytic psychotherapy trainees, this is not true for every school or professional discipline. Many psychotherapists and counsellors are trained within a much more broadly defined, eclectic, model of practice and supervision. As Nelson (1978) comments with respect to his survey of psychotherapy trainees' preferences regarding supervision:

> The results of the present study indicate more similarities than differences in the preferences of psychotherapy trainees from different professional disciplines and levels of training. However, the differences revealed suggest that psychotherapy supervision should not be conceptualized as a fixed collection of techniques equally applicable across professional disciplines and levels of training.
>
> (1978: 548)[2]

Nelson's research suggests that supervisors should be sufficiently flexible to modify their approach to supervision according to the needs of the supervisee. The necessity for flexibility in the supervisory relationship is also acknowledged by Pedder (1986), who considers that supervision has a function somewhere between therapy and education. Precisely where on the spectrum between therapy and education supervision is to be located will, in his opinion, vary according to the stage of professional development reached by the supervisee. Moreover, as it is Pedder's view that both psychotherapy and supervision share the common aim of promoting growth in people, he suggests that 'Just as with psychotherapy itself, the level of therapy will vary with the developmental level of the patient. A more disturbed patient may need more directive support; a healthier patient needs much less' (Pedder 1986: 2). The extent to which supervision is didactic or therapeutic in orientation, and the values and theories underlying the relative importance attached to these roles, are issues I shall return to later in this chapter. Before doing so, however, I wish to define the term 'supervision' and outline some essential functions of a supervisor.

Some functions of a supervisor

The word 'supervision' is generally applied to situations in which one person inspects or oversees another's work from a position of authority. As Williams (1992: 96) comments, 'A supervisor in common usage is the boss, the person who is to be obeyed, the person who tells us what to do and is responsible for our actions.' As this definition tends to imply an intrinsically authoritarian relationship, and conflicts with the actual function of clinical supervisors, more 'user-friendly' terms such as consultant, facilitator or mentor have increasingly entered the therapeutic vocabulary to describe the role and function of the supervisor. Although in some organizations a supervisor may have a managerial role in relation to those whom they supervise, when applied to therapeutic work the word supervision is generally used to describe the process by which a therapist or trainee receives support and guidance in order to ensure the needs of the client are understood and responded to appropriately. This process encompasses a number of functions concerned with monitoring, developing and supporting individuals in their helping or counselling role (British Association for Counselling 1990). To this end, supervision is usually concerned with reducing the anxiety of the therapist, improving the service to the client, evolving fresh and creative approaches to clinical problems, increasing the trainee's or therapist's self-awareness and helping them develop an independent professional identity (Kaslow 1986). As such, supervision is widely regarded as an essential element in the training and continuing education of mental-health-related professionals, including: art therapists (Edwards 1993), counsellors (Dryden and Thorne 1991), clinical and educational psychologists (Pilgrim and Treacher 1992; Lunt and Pomerantz 1993), psychiatric nurses (Simms 1993), psychotherapists (Ashurst 1993) and social workers (Ford and Jones 1987; Munson 1993).

Despite this broad consensus concerning its importance, notable differences and disagreements exist concerning the means by which the generally agreed aims of supervision might best be accomplished. Numerous models, styles and approaches to supervision exist, and these differences both inform and influence the ways the term is now used and understood. For example, supervision may be provided individually by a more experienced therapist (Greben

1991) or arranged on a peer group basis (Bonnivier 1992). In addition, it may or may not involve the use of audio- or videotapes (Rubinstein and Hammond 1982; Aveline 1992) or a formal assessment or evaluation of the trainee's or therapist's ability to conduct therapeutic work (Davis 1989). In family work supervision may be 'live' and take place during the therapy session itself in conjunction with the use of a one-way screen or the so called 'bug in the ear' (Kingston and Smith 1983).

At the present time, and in all probability for the foreseeable future, the question 'who is the ideal supervisor?' is one likely to elicit only a partisan reply (Carifio and Hess 1987). The preferred ways of working of supervisors are typically influenced less by the available research on supervision (Lambert 1980) than by the way they themselves have been supervised; usually, though not always, during the period of their training (Guest and Beutler 1988). The role of supervision within training – its quality, theoretical orientation and mode of delivery – not only influences the subsequent clinical work of therapists, but also appears to influence the approach taken to the supervision of others later in their careers (Watkins 1991). Moreover, as few clinicians undertake any formal training in supervision prior to assuming the role, considerable variation may be expected, and is often found, between supervisors concerning the ways in which they function and perceive their role (Bernard 1981). In practice, supervisors often function, even within the same professional discipline or organization, in very different ways. Though this may not necessarily prove problematic it can, as Mollon (1989a: 7) comments with respect to clinical psychology, contribute to difficulties in establishing 'an authentic professional identity'. In situations where very different theoretical models are being utilized in order to make sense of the material presented in supervision, the mismatch between supervisor and trainee may, as Pilgrim and Treacher (1992: 125) observe, be 'potentially very damaging'.

Tensions between the training and developmental role of the supervisor

An important aspect of supervision is monitoring and controlling the admission of trainees to a profession. Outside the training context supervisors may also have managerial or administrative responsibilities for those they supervise or have a role in regulating the conduct of qualified practitioners: that is, with ensuring clinicians maintain appropriate standards of competence and professionalism. Both the British Association for Counselling and the United Kingdom Council for Psychotherapy, for example, require members to actively monitor their own competence and have complaints procedures that enable sanctions to be imposed against therapists considered to be practising unprofessionally (British Association for Counselling 1990; Pokorny 1995). One obvious tension in such situations arises from the potential conflict of interests between the supervisor's need to know that standards are being maintained and the clinician's need to demonstrate that this is actually the case. If the demands of the institution or organization place excessive pressure upon the therapist or trainee to demonstrate that their work is efficient, and in many cases cost-effective, opportunities for learning, emotional support and creativity may be replaced by defensive manoeuvres such as denial, withdrawal and ritualized forms of service delivery:

> The more staff are encouraged to rely on so-called rational decision making tools, procedural manuals and routinized service delivery methods the more they stop thinking for themselves. These kinds of blinkered responses tend to limit open-minded problem exploration: narrow and superficial discussion in supervision sessions can trap supervisor and supervised into a happy conclusion that all is inspected and under control.
>
> (Coulshed 1990: 42)

The administrative or gate-keeping functions of supervisors usually involve, with varying degrees of formality, an assessment or evaluation of the therapist's or trainee's therapeutic competence: supervisors are invested with a significant amount of power. In addition to this, supervisors may also enjoy considerable authority and influence by virtue of their experience or position within the training organization. As a consequence, the relationship between supervisor and supervisee is, in most cases, a hierarchical and unequal one (Jones 1989). No matter how sensitively this issue is handled, such inequality may result in some measure of conflict; conflict which has as its focal point factors involving privacy (Betcher and Zinberg 1988), cross-cultural issues (Batten 1990), ethical issues (Bond 1990), or the fear of being harshly judged (Lubin 1985). If not adequately addressed within the supervisory relationship, these conflicts may inhibit the supervisee's ability, need or desire to learn (Scaife 1993).

The very real inequalities of power in the supervisory relationship may be heightened by transference issues arising out of past good or bad experiences of being in similar power relationships, with parents or teachers, for example (Salzberger-Wittenberg *et al.* 1992). Powerful transferential feelings may be mobilized with respect to the hope or fear that the supervisor will be the fountain of knowledge and wisdom, a provider and comforter, an object of admiration or envy, a judge or some other figure of authority. A figure who may – in phantasy if not in fact – be perceived as excessively punitive or benevolent and consequently denigrated or idealized (Brightman 1984). It is, of course, also necessary to note here that transferences do not simply flow one way. Supervisors, too, may experience powerful emotional responses in the supervisory situation. Responses that may, or may not, be considered helpful in facilitating the supervision process (Searles 1965; Doehrman 1976).

Exposition of the didactic and the experiential models of supervision

As will, I trust, be clear from the foregoing discussion, the practice of supervision is subject to considerable variation regarding its focus, organization and theoretical orientation. While there may be general agreement about the aims of supervision – that it is intended to help therapists address the needs of their clients – how best these aspirations might be met remains both a debatable point and a source of potential conflict within the supervisory relationship itself. Despite this, two main models of supervision have evolved, and it is either between or around these that the many and varied styles of supervision, currently on offer are situated. Many forms of supervision, however, like the 'double matrix model' advocated by Hawkins and Shohet (1989), aim to integrate and combine elements of both.

The first of these is the didactic model of supervision in which the mode of learning is primarily rational, concerned with conscious thought processes, and in which considerable importance is attached to the teaching of theory and technique (Levine and Tilker 1974; Forsyth and Ivey 1980; Mead 1990). By contrast, the second model of supervision tends to be more subjective and experiential in nature. Within this model the emphasis in supervision is upon the trainee's or therapist's feelings and unconscious emotional responses to the client (Gauthier 1984; Casement 1985, 1990; Gorkin 1987). What is in many respects so remarkable about this contemporary separation of functions is how closely these two distinctly different approaches to supervision echo the disagreement that emerged in the very earliest days of organized psychoanalytic training between the Hungarian and Viennese schools of thought. In essence, this disagreement concerned the respective roles and functions of the control analysis and the training analysis, the former term referring to the supervised clinical work conducted by an analyst during his or her training, the latter to the training analyst's own psychoanalysis.

The distinction to be made between the control analysis and training analysis, and more subtly between the terms *Kontrollanalyse* and *Analysenkontrolle*, lay at the heart of disagreements over the nature and content of psychoanalytic training which initially surfaced at the Four-Countries Conference in 1935 (Glover 1935).[3] The Hungarian school stressed the importance of the training analysis and argued that the therapist's countertransference feelings were most effectively addressed there. That, in effect, the therapist's own analysis would serve as supervision (Kovacs 1936). The Viennese psychoanalysts, on the other hand, maintained that the candidate's personal analyst should not supervise their work. Thus, the function of the control analysis was to enable the training analyst to work with someone who would instruct and not analyse them, the aim being to help the training analyst avoid the mistakes beginners usually make (Bibring 1937). Any personal issues that emerged in this essentially didactic exercise were to be referred to the training analyst.

Eventually a compromise was reached regarding this issue, with the Hungarian analysts conceding that instruction, information and advice should not be avoided, and the Viennese analysts acknowledging that countertransference issues might sometimes need to be addressed in the control analysis. However, as DeBell (1963: 552) notes, 'It is striking that there is no extensive refutation of Kovacs' position . . . with little further trace in the literature, he [Bibring] appears to have carried the field.' Despite this, and the subsequent institutionalizing of both personal therapy or analysis and supervision as essential components of psychoanalytic and psychotherapy training throughout the world, the issue of where, when and how to draw the boundary between supervision and therapy, and between the didactic and developmental aspects of supervision has, as numerous commentators have observed, never been fully resolved (Ekstein 1960; Schlessinger 1966; Haesler 1993). Balint (1948) was particularly critical of the psychoanalytic training system as it developed, and argued that the decision taken in 1947 by the London Institute of Psycho-Analysis that different analysts must each either undertake the candidate's personal analysis or the supervision of their cases was more the result of dogma than clear thinking. This decision does not, however, appear to have been rigorously enforced and it is interesting to note that Balint continued to supervise the first case of his analysand, with the approval of the Training Committee of the London Institute, from 1947 until his death.

The psychoanalytic legacy

The complex issue of whether, or to what extent, supervision should be 'therapeutic' in so far as it pays attention to, and possibly seeks to alleviate, difficult or problematic feelings therapists or trainees have in response to their work continues to be debated. Indeed much of the literature already cited in this chapter is, in one way or another, concerned with this very issue. Nevertheless, the prevailing trend within psychoanalytic training today, as with training in most other psychotherapeutic or mental health professions, is to emphasize the teaching function of supervision and to downplay its therapeutic dimension. Following the decision to make a training analysis obligatory for every candidate wishing to train as an analyst, initially taken at the 1922 Congress of the International Psychoanalytical Association, most psychotherapy training courses currently running in the UK advocate that the appropriate place in which the therapist is best able to learn about the nature of his or her personality, habitual responses to others and areas of conflict is in personal therapy (Pedder 1989; Aveline 1990). As Wilson and Barkham (1994: 55–6) observe, 'The marked exception to this legacy is the cognitive-behavioural paradigm, which has dominated clinical and academic psychology.'

However, although it has long since been recognized that forms of clinical practice which are psychotherapeutic in their orientation cannot be taught or supervised in a purely didactic manner, the question of how best to support or help the trainee or clinician address the emotional impact their work may have upon them remains problematic. This is an issue, moreover, that is as relevant to general practitioners, psychiatric nurses, social workers and members of many other caring professions as it is to psychoanalysts, psychotherapists and counsellors. This dilemma may, as Mollon (1989b) suggests, be particularly acute in those professions such as clinical psychology which emphasize the importance of research and technical procedures in clinical work. By its very nature, the work undertaken by all these professional groups involves, amongst other potential sources of stress, close contact with emotional pain and suffering. The recognition that this may lead to 'burnout' (Ross et al. 1989), with the consequent loss of empathy or sensitivity towards the client, is a major contributory factor in the increasing attention now paid to supervision within many organizations.

Though they are sometimes advocated, counselling or psychotherapy are rarely routinely provided for mental health professionals in order to help them address the emotional impact of their work and personal consequences this may have (Woodmansey 1991). Whereas further training which involves the trainee entering therapy themselves may be an option for some, at present the majority of psychotherapy courses tend to be highly specialized, expensive, time-consuming and located in London or the south of England. Furthermore, as the various forms of psychotherapy and counselling available outside the National Health Service are inclined to be equally expensive and difficult to access, the option of entering therapy as an adjunct, or even prior, to working with individuals experiencing mental health problems is also limited.

The work of Michael Balint is of particular interest in relation to this issue. Faced with the problem of helping social workers become aware of, and sensitive to, unconscious processes when dealing with their clients' marital problems, and without being able to offer them personal analysis, Balint and his wife Enid based their approach on the Hungarian system of supervision (Balint 1964). Modifying the method to employ a group-based approach to exploring countertransference issues the social workers were encouraged to report freely, in a manner very similar to 'free association', about their experiences with clients. This method was further developed by Balint for training general practitioners in psychotherapy at the Tavistock Clinic in London. For Balint, psychotherapy was not theoretical knowledge but a personal skill, the acquisition of which consisted of more than learning something new. It also entailed a limited, though considerable change of personality (Balint 1964). Though something of an iconoclast, Balint's influence on psychotherapy in the UK has, as Pedder (1986) notes, been considerable. Balint's work appears to have proved especially inspirational to psychotherapists wishing to develop training schemes in geographically isolated areas where suitably qualified personnel may be in short supply (Freeman 1991) or those who, like the Sheffield-based psychoanalyst Colin Woodmansey, questioned the value of drawing any distinction between teaching and supervision, or between supervision and personal therapy (Woodmansey 1987).

Concluding remarks

While the influence of psychoanalysis on the development of supervision has been substantial, and is arguably the dominant one, other factors have clearly played a part in shaping current theory and practice. Due acknowledgement must, therefore, be made to the unique contributions of Carl Rogers (1957) and Norman Kagan (1980) amongst many others to the training and supervision of therapists. Rogers' contribution to the field of psychotherapy and counselling has been, as Villas-Boas Bowen (1986: 291) argues, primarily through emphasizing the capacity of both clients and therapists for 'self-regulation, self-direction, and self-determination'. Kagan's work, by contrast, demonstrates the ways in which the creative use of relatively cheap audiovisual equipment within the supervision process can offer therapists opportunities to learn about their interactions with clients in ways undreamt of in the early days of organized psychoanalytic training.

Though now recognized as an essential component in the training and continuing education of therapists and mental health professionals, strong disagreements nevertheless remain regarding the appropriateness of the various approaches to supervision advocated in the literature. For the neophyte therapist or supervisor this diversity may result in a mismatch of expectations or confusion regarding roles and responsibilities. That clinicians undertake some training in supervision as part of, or subsequent to, their basic training, may prove helpful in reducing the likely risk of such unfortunate, but I suspect all too common, experiences. The question remains, however, 'what should the content of such a training be?'

In practice, different professions are inclined to answer this question according to the values and theories upon which their clinical practice is based. Thus, supervisors whose training and clinical practice is firmly rooted in psychoanalysis attach considerably more importance to unconscious processes and free association than do therapists from other traditions. Whilst this may be an appropriate way of training and supervising therapists within a particular discipline – although even here, as already noted, considerable disagreement may be found – in some settings therapists from one profession may be routinely found supervising therapists from another. With respect to my own profession, for example, according to a survey published by the British Association of Art Therapists and the Manufacturing, Science and Finance Trade Union (BAAT and MSF 1990: 4.3) art therapists tend to be supervised by practitioners from a wide range of professional disciplines, including occupational therapists, psychiatrists, psychotherapists, psychologists and social workers. The actual percentage of art therapists in the National Health Service receiving sole supervision from other art therapists was only 27.9 per cent. Experience suggests that the art therapy profession is by no means unique in this respect.

It is not my intention here to suggest that multi-disciplinary supervision is necessarily problematic. Indeed it may, on the contrary, be very valuable. My concern is that clinicians who are unsure of their own professional identity may uncritically imitate the supervisory styles of more experienced practitioners from other disciplines. They may also, as previously noted with respect to clinical psychology, experience severe difficulty in reconciling the different approaches to supervision they encounter during or after their training. In addition to acknowledging the need for practitioners to develop supervisory styles that match the requirements of their own professional discipline, there is, I believe, also an argument in favour of developing multi-disciplinary training courses in supervision that consist of more than relatively brief, experientially-based introductions to the subject. Valuable though such short courses may be, rarely do they offer the opportunity to examine in depth some of the more complex issues and questions arising in the supervisory relationship. Some of these issues have already been touched upon in this chapter. Others might include addressing such questions as, 'To what extent might either the "internalized supervisor" or video camera intrude into the privacy of the therapeutic relationship?', and 'How might we best approach and resolve the dilemma, often experienced in supervision by both supervisors and supervisees alike, between the client's needs and the therapist's needs?' In approaching these questions openly such a course ought to acknowledge the many unresolved issues in the historical development of supervision. If supervision, like history itself, is to be considered an art, it is one that must also seek to distinguish fact from fiction.

Notes

1 PsycLIT, the main database for books and articles on psychology, psychiatry and related disciplines, for example, lists 1,752 references to supervision in journals published between January 1987 and November 1994, and a further 390 references in books published over the same period.
2 The list of preferred supervisor role behaviours elicited by Nelson included, in order of preference, encouraging the trainees to develop their own style of therapy, providing trainees with opportunities to explore their feelings towards clients and their problems, encouraging experimentation and teaching techniques (Nelson 1978: 546).
3 According to Laplanche and Pontalis (1988: 90), it is suggested the term *Kontrollanalyse* be used to denote the analysis of the candidate's countertransference *vis-à-vis* his patient, and *Analysenkontrolle* the supervision of his analysis of the patient.

References

Ashurst, P. (1993) Supervision of the beginning therapist. *British Journal of Psychotherapy*, 10(2): 170–7.
Aveline, M. (1990) The training and supervision of individual therapists, in W. Dryden (ed.) *Individual Therapy: A handbook.* Milton Keynes: Open University Press.
Aveline, M. (1992) The use of audio and videotape recordings of therapy sessions in the supervision and practice of dynamic psychotherapy. *British Journal of Psychotherapy*, 8(4): 347–57.
BAAT [British Association of Art Therapists] and MSF (1990) *Survey of Conditions of Service of Registered Art Therapists.* Brighton: British Association of Art Therapists.
Balint, M. (1948) On the psycho-analytic training system. *International Journal of Psycho-Analysis*, 29(3): 163–73.
Balint, M. (1964) *The Doctor, His Patient and the Illness.* London: Pitman.
Batten, C. (1990) Dilemmas of crosscultural psychotherapy supervision. *British Journal of Psychotherapy*, 7(2): 129–40.
Bernard, J.M. (1981) Inservice training for clinical supervisors. *Professional Psychology*, 12(6), December: 740–8.
Betcher, W.R. and Zinberg, N.E. (1988) Supervision and privacy in psychotherapy training. *American Journal of Psychiatry*, 147(7), July: 796–803.
Bibring, E. (1937) Methods and techniques of control analysis. *International Journal of Psycho-Analysis*, 18: 369–70.
Bond, T. (1990) Counselling supervision – ethical issues. *Counselling*, May: 43–6.
Bonnivier, J.F. (1992) A peer supervision group. Put countertransference to work. *Journal of Psychosocial Nursing*, 30(5): 5–8.
Brightman, B.K. (1984) Narcissistic issues in the training experience of the psychotherapist. *International Journal of Psychoanalytic Psychotherapy*, 10: 293–317.
British Association for Counselling (1990) *Code of Ethics and Practice for Counsellors.* Rugby: British Association for Counselling.
Carifio, M.S. and Hess, A.K. (1987) Who is the ideal supervisor? *Professional Psychologist: Research and Practice*, 18(3): 244–50.
Casement, P. (1985) *On Learning from the Patient.* London: Routledge.
Casement, P. (1990) *Further Learning from the Patient.* London: Routledge.
Coulshed, V. (1990) Soapbox. *Social Work Today*, 11 October: 42.
Davis, J. (1989) Issues in the evaluation of counsellors by supervisors. *Counselling*, 69, August: 31–7.
DeBell, D.E. (1963) A critical digest of the literature on psychoanalytic supervision, *Journal of the American Psychoanalytic Association*, 11: 546–75.
Doehrman, M.J. (1976) Parallel processes in supervision and psychotherapy. *Bulletin of the Menninger Clinic*, 40(1), January: 9-104.
Dryden, W. and Thorne, B. (1991) *Training and Supervision for Counselling in Action.* London: Sage.
Edwards, D. (1993) Learning about feelings. The role of supervision in art therapy training. *The Arts in Psychotherapy*, 20: 213–22.
Ekstein, R. (1960) A historical survey of the teaching of psychoanalytic technique. *Journal of the American Psychoanalytic Association*, 8: 500–16.
Ford, K. and Jones, A.I. (1987) *Student Supervision.* London: Macmillan.

Forsyth, D.R. and Ivey, A.E. (1980) Microtraining. An approach to differential supervision, in A.K. Hess (ed.) *Psychotherapy Supervision: Theory, Research, and Practice*. New York: John Wiley and Sons.

Freeman, T. (1991) Hobson's Choice. Personal analysis and supervision in the training of psychoanalytic psychotherapists. *British Journal of Psychotherapy*, 8(2): 202–5.

Gauthier, M. (1984) Countertransference and supervision. A discussion of some dynamics from the point of view of the supervisee. *Canadian Journal of Psychiatry*, 29(6), October: 513–9.

Glover, E. (ed.) (1935) Bulletin of the International Psycho-Analytical Association (Four-Countries Conference). *International Journal of Psycho-Analysis*, 16: 505–9.

Gorkin, M. (1987) *The Uses of Countertransference*. New York: Jason Aronson.

Greben, S.E. (1991) Interpersonal aspects of the supervision of individual psychotherapy. *American Journal of Psychotherapy*, XLV(3), July: 306–16.

Guest, P.D. and Beutler, L.E. (1988) Impact of psychotherapy supervision on therapist orientation and values. *Journal of Consulting and Clinical Psychology*, 56(5): 653–8.

Haesler, L. (1993) Adequate distance in the relationship between supervisor and supervisee. *International Journal of Psycho-Analysis*, 74: 547–55.

Hawkins, P. and Shohet, R. (1989) *Supervision in the Helping Professions*. Milton Keynes: Open University Press.

Holloway, E.L. (1984) Outcome evaluation in supervision research. *The Counseling Psychologist*, 12(4): 167–74.

Jones, R. (1989) Supervision. A choice between equals? *British Journal of Psychotherapy*, 5(4): 505–11.

Kagan, N. (1980) Influencing human interaction. Eighteen years with IPR, in A.K. Hess (ed.) *Psychotherapy Supervision: Theory, research, and practice*, New York: John Wiley and Sons, Inc.

Kaslow, F.W. (ed.) (1986) *Supervision and Training: Models, dilemmas, and challenges*. New York: Haworth.

Kingston, P. and Smith, D. (1983) Preparation for live consultation and live supervision when working without a one-way screen. *Journal of Family Therapy*, 5: 219–33.

Kovacs, V. (1936) Training and control-analysis. *International Journal of Psycho-Analysis*, 18: 346–54.

Lambert, M.J. (1980) Research and the supervisory process, in A.K. Hess (ed.) *Psychotherapy Supervision: Theory, research, and practice*. New York: John Wiley and Sons, Inc.

Laplanche, J. and Pontalis, J.-B. (1988) *The Language of Psycho-Analysis*. London: Karnac Books and the Institute of Psycho-Analysis.

Levine, F.M. and Tilker, H.A. (1974) A behaviour modification approach to supervision of psychotherapy. *Psychotherapy: Theory, research and practice*, 11(2): 182–8.

Lubin, M. (1985) Another source of danger for psychotherapists. The supervisory introject. *International Journal of Psychoanalytic Psychotherapy*, 10: 25–45.

Lunt, I. and Pomerantz, M. (1993) Supervision and psychologists' professional work. *Educational and Child Psychology*, 10(2): 3–89.

Marshall, R.J. (1993) Perspectives on supervision. Tea and/or supervision. *Modern Psychoanalysis*, 18(1): 45–57.

Mead, E.D. (1990) *Effective Supervision: A task-oriented model for the mental health professions*. New York: Brunner/Mazel.

Mollon, P. (1989a) Narcissus, Oedipus and the psychologist's fraudulent identity. *Clinical Psychology Forum*, 23: 7–11.

Mollon, P. (1989b) Anxiety, supervision and a space for thinking. Some narcissistic perils for clinical psychologists in learning psychotherapy. *British Journal of Medical Psychology*, 62: 113–22.

Munson, C.E. (1993) *Clinical Social Work Supervision*. New York: Haworth.

Nelson, G.L. (1978) Psychotherapy supervision from the trainee's point of view. A survey of preferences. *Professional Psychology*, November: 539–50.

Pedder, J. (1986) Reflections on the theory and practice of supervision. *Psychoanalytic Psychotherapy*, 2(1): 1–12.

Pedder, J. (1989) Courses in psychotherapy. Evolution and current trends. *British Journal of Psychotherapy*, 6(2): 203–21.

Pilgrim, D. and Treacher, A. (1992) *Clinical Psychology Observed*. London: Routledge.

Pokorny, M. (1995) History of the United Kingdom Council for Psychotherapy. *British Journal of Psychotherapy*, 11(3): 415–21.

Rogers, C. (1957) Training individuals to engage in the therapeutic process, in C.R. Strother (ed.) *Psychology and Mental Health*. Washington, DC: American Psychological Association.

Ross, R.R., Altmaier, E.M. and Russell, D.W. (1989) Job stress, social support, and burnout amongst counseling center staff. *Journal of Counseling Psychology*, 36(4): 464–70.

Rubinstein, M. and Hammond, D. (1982) The use of videotape in psychotherapy supervision, in M. Blumenfield (ed.) *Applied Supervision in Psychotherapy*. New York: Grune & Stratton.

Salzberger-Wittenberg, I., Henry, G. and Osborne, E. (1992) *The Emotional Experience of Learning and Teaching*. London: Routledge.

Scaife, J.M. (1993) Application of a general supervision framework. Creating a context of co-operation. *Educational and Child Psychology*, 10(2): 61–72.

Schlessinger, N. (1966) Supervision of psychotherapy. A critical review of the literature. *Archives of General Psychiatry*, 14, August: 129–34.

Searles, H.F. (1965) *Collected Papers on Schizophrenia and Related Subjects*. London: Hogarth Press.

Simms, J. (1993) Supervision, in H. Wright and M. Giddey (eds) *Mental Health Nursing*. London: Chapman Hall.

Villas-Boas Bowen, M.C. (1986) Personality differences and person-centred supervision. *Person-Centred Review*, 1(3): 291–309.

Watkins, E.C. (1991) Reflections on the preparation of psychotherapy supervisors. *Journal of Clinical Psychology*, 47(6), November: 145–7.

Williams, I.D.I. (1992) Supervision. A new word is desperately needed. *Counselling*, May: 96.

Wilson, J.E. and Barkham, M. (1994) A practitioner–scientist approach to psychotherapy process and outcome research, in P. Clarkson and M. Pokorny (eds) *The Handbook of Psychotherapy*. London: Routledge.

Woodmansey, A.C. (1987) What's wrong with psychotherapy? *British Journal of Clinical and Social Psychiatry*, 5(3): 73–5.

Woodmansey, A.C. (1991) How a staff counselling service can help social service agencies. *British Journal of Clinical and Social Psychiatry*, 8(2): 36–8.

3

SUPERVISION AS A SPACE FOR THINKING

Phil Mollon

Introduction

Somebody called a 'supervisee' comes to someone called a 'supervisor'. Why do they do so? What goes on between them? What are the functions of supervision? Two common functions are: (1) transmission of information from supervisor to supervisee; and (2) monitoring of the trainee's work to ensure its safety, efficacy, consistency with policy, etc. Both of these concern the role of supervisor as authority. Trainees of an authoritarian disposition, or an authoritarian professional background (such as nursing) frequently have difficulty in conceiving of any other function of the supervisor that is not to do with authority. However, it is a third function, which is nothing to do with authority, that particularly interests me. This is the creation of a *space for thinking* (Mollon 1989). In this chapter, I describe what this space consists of and indicate those factors which facilitate and those which interfere with this space for thinking.

Left- and right-brain thinking

What kind of thinking am I referring to? I am not concerned with a very focused, linear, 'left-brain' problem-solving kind of activity, but with reflective thinking which is more akin to 'rêverie'. This involves mulling over, sifting through impressions without hurriedly coming to conclusions; it is free-associative rather than directed, allowing thought to germinate and develop in the mind and in the discourse between participants. It is a kind of thinking rarely taught at universities, particularly not on science-based courses (including psychology and medicine), a cognitive activity which may draw more from right-brain hemispheric functioning. Although the neuropsychological evidence is ambiguous, there are clear suggestions that the right hemisphere is concerned with unconscious information-processing and especially emotional information-processing, and that it apprehends the world in a holistic, intuitive and non-linear manner – whereas the left hemisphere processes information sequentially, verbally and 'rationally'. This distinction was first proposed by Ornstein (1970). Many popular and speculative formulations have followed, a notable contribution being Edwards's (1979) application to drawing – but the general idea is given some credence by serious scientists (e.g. Springer and Deutsch 1989).

A further dichotomy that I draw is between learning from research and learning from experience. We can learn much that is important from research and from reading research reports – e.g. about techniques and processes in psychotherapy and about what is efficacious and what is not. We can also gain important learning from reading or from being taught in a classroom, but all of this is quite different from, and no substitute for, learning from experience. To learn from experience we must allow ourselves to *have* an experience, to become aware of it and then to think reflectively about it. The awareness of the experience with the patient and the experience in supervision is not instant and complete, but gradually emerges, although sometimes with flashes of clarity. At times the supervisee's emotional experience of the patient is in the foreground, for example, if the patient is a very stormy or threatening character with a borderline personality. Often, however, the therapist's experience of the patient is not in the foreground of awareness but exists at the periphery of consciousness. Part of what happens in supervision is that the peripheral elements of experience shift into the foreground of awareness.

Example: the self-contained flat

A counsellor talked of feeling that her patient, a man who lived with his elderly mother and had a very limited life with no work and few friends, was very 'stuck', not making any progress in the therapy. She also felt 'stuck' and frustrated in her attempts to work with him. She described how she had tried various approaches to help him bring about change, including attempts to engage with child parts of his personality through offering drawing materials and sand play. After listening to some minutes of this account, the supervisor commented that perhaps the patient basically did not want to change, but might in fact be very invested in maintaining the status quo and in resisting the counsellor's attempts to reach him emotionally. In response the counsellor recalled a dream the patient had presented some weeks previously. In the dream the patient is in a self-contained flat which contains everything he needs; there is one small window; he looks through the window and sees children trying to get in; he shoots at the children to drive them back. The meaning of the dream was startlingly obvious: it was clearly a description of his preferred mental state of narcissistic self-containment and his efforts to ward off the counsellor's efforts to engage with child parts of his personality; these child parts had been projected into the counsellor who, in response to her identification with these, had been trying to approach him with play materials. Until talking about her experience in supervision the counsellor could not fully *identify* her experience and could not link this with the patient's dream. By empathizing with both the patient's experience and the counsellor's experience, the supervisor could bring about an understanding which encompassed what was happening *between* patient and counsellor; it could then be understood that patient and counsellor were at that moment pursuing quite opposing agendas.

Example: the karate man

As the therapist's experience is mulled over in supervision the interactive *projective* processes in the therapy may become apparent. These are the experiences which the patient actively, but unconsciously, endeavours to create in the therapist. Again these are difficult for the therapist to become aware of without the reflective space of supervision.

A psychologist, Dr G., talked to me about a patient he had been seeing for some weeks – a man prone to panic attacks and who happened to be a karate expert. From time to time the man had been involved in episodes of violence. The patient's background was that his grandfather was a high-ranking naval officer who completely dominated his mother and his father, who was also in the navy but at a much more junior level. The patient grew up in this very aggressive military atmosphere. He tended to proclaim his dislike of all men and his preference for female company. After an initial meeting with the psychologist he had reported to one of Dr G's colleagues that he hated Dr G's guts and did not want to see him again. However, he did return for a further appointment. Dr G began to feel extremely uncomfortable with the way that the patient was looking at him during the sessions and found himself using humour as a way of relieving the intense atmosphere. The patient seemed to like this very much and subsequently spoke highly of Dr G to this other colleague.

Part of Dr G's work with the patient had been cognitive-behavioural, helping him to find ways of managing his panic attacks. Rather to Dr G's surprise the patient seemed to benefit from this approach. Then Dr G described an episode in which the patient had been enraged by another man and had set off to beat him up; however, on encountering this man and seeing his overt terror, the patient had felt he could not follow through his aggression and had then himself experienced a panic attack, which he had been able to manage using the advice Dr G had given him. I pointed out the projective processes involved here: the patient grew up in a harsh and bullying military atmosphere, intimidated by his grandfather; he had attempted to deal with his own terror by becoming able to intimidate others; if this projection failed, such as when his empathy prevailed, he was then faced with his own terror and experienced a panic attack. As we talked about this, Dr G remarked that he was suddenly aware that he is, in fact, very frightened of the patient – afraid that the patient could suddenly turn against him and assault him. He pointed to a recent incident in a session: the patient had reported that he was cutting out his addiction to tranquillizers and that he had decided he no longer needed to carry a tablet around with him; Dr G commented, 'It was as if he was a big boy now!' When Dr G had questioned him about whether this was a good idea, the patient had become very anxious and had reported an impulse to attack Dr G. It was clear that he had experienced Dr G's comment as an attempt to knock him down and make him feel like a frightened little boy again and that this had triggered the old pattern of using his aggression in the service of projecting fear into the other. Two distinct modes of relationship were apparent: there was the old pattern in which one man attempts to intimidate the other, based upon the experience with his grandfather; there was also the new and more benign constructive relationship represented by the patient's experience with Dr G, reflecting his longing for a closer relationship of the kind he had not experienced in his original family. Through supervision, Dr G became aware of his experience of the patient and of the patient's experience of him. Through reflecting upon the experience, as well as upon the narratives of the sessional material, the underlying meaning emerged. We could then see what kind of experience the patient was fearing and what kind of experience he was seeking.

Functions of the supervisor in building the space

The supervisor has the advantage of hearing about both the patient and the therapist. To that extent the supervisor's consciousness of the material and of the interaction in the therapy can be larger than that of the therapist. An analogy can be drawn with the concept of the 'global workspace' developed by the cognitive psychologist Bernard Baars (1988). Baars argues that the function of consciousness is to facilitate communication between information-processing systems – the global workspace of consciousness being like a kind of bulletin board or broadcasting centre where information and messages are made 'public'. Supervision can be seen as providing a 'global workspace' between the minds of the therapist and supervisor, the full consciousness existing in the space between them. By the supervisor's offering the function of listener, the therapist is invited to speak of his/her experience. Until speaking, the therapist may be relatively unaware of his/her unarticulated experience; by listening, the supervisor hears the great variety of different impressions, feelings and fantasies of the therapist; by reflecting these back, the therapist's consciousness (global workspace) is enlarged. The notion of the enlarged global workspace resulting from supervision may be compared with a similar but contrasting concept of the 'mutilation of psychic space', described by Gear et al. (1981) as a mental defence used by narcissistic patients which involves a narrowing of the field of consciousness.

The supervisor may also be regarded as providing a number of *selfobject* functions. This concept, developed originally by Kohut (1971, 1977) refers to those functions of the other, most notably the provision of empathy, which are necessary for a person's sense of well-being and coherence of self. Grotstein (1981) presents a concept of a particular selfobject function which he terms the 'background object of primary identification'. He sees this as to do with the sense of being *backed up*, supported as if from *underneath*, having a *background* constancy; certainly the quiet reflective consistency of the supervisor provides this function, one which may gradually be internalized as the therapist becomes his/her own supervisor.

Thinking, not thinking, dreaming and waking up

Not all that masquerades as thinking is in fact real thinking. The analyst who wrote most extensively about this was Wilfred Bion. He arrived at his theories of thinking through his observations of the thought disorders of very disturbed psychotic patients. In attempting to conceptualize their thought (and quasi-thought) processes, he postulated a psychotic part of the mind which is intolerant of thought and painful experience. Instead of tolerating an experience and allowing thought to grow around it, the psychotic part of the mind will attempt to function as an expulsive muscle, getting rid of the experience rather than thinking about it. As a result, the psychotic mind cannot learn from experience because it cannot tolerate experience. In this sense we are perhaps all psychotic to varying extents. Bion then turned his attention to the analyst's capacity to think, drawing attention to the ways in which desires to know and understand prematurely, as well as desires to cure or to get rid of the patient's pain, may interfere with being receptive to new experience. Premature quasi-understanding, based upon familiar formulas, may be substituted for the more frightening and unknown truth of the patient. Bion counselled analysts to listen without memory or desire, to observe 'without irritable reaching after fact and reason', his quotation from Keats describing the capacity for 'negative capability' (Bion 1967). I think the prototype of the kind of thinking that Bion had in mind is dreaming – a right-brain, non-linear and non-logical mental activity which is concerned with processing emotional experience. The meanings of dreams are of course condensed. To unravel their meaning the images and scenes must be allowed to activate the associative networks of the mind. After reflecting associatively about a dream for some time, its latent meaning may become clear – or it may not. The material of a psychotherapy session is sometimes like this. Its meaning must be unravelled. It must be listened to with the right brain, left and right hemispheres must communicate and coordinate in order to understand and speak about its meaning.

Example: the two robots

Wendy, a community psychiatric nurse, consulted me because she was unhappy about her work with an agoraphobic patient, a 26-year-old woman living with her parents. She was unclear exactly what it was that she was uncomfortable about. The patient appeared to be making good progress. Wendy had taken over the patient from a colleague who had left and who had been working on behaviour therapy principles. The behavioural work had been going well. Wendy spoke freely about many aspects of the situation. We considered, for example, whether Wendy really did not like inheriting a case and being asked to work behaviourally, which was not her preferred mode. Wendy went on to speak of her dislike of the patient's parents and the excessively clean and tidy state of the house, and of the lack of privacy in the open plan setting. We identified that the patient seemed compliant, wanting to please Wendy. However, the crucial point emerged when Wendy recalled that on one occasion, on leaving the patient's house, she had thought to herself angrily 'I've had enough of this!' She had noticed this as an unusual thought, without being clear what it was that she had had enough of. Having recalled this, we could then begin to see that this thought, and the accompanying anger, reflected Wendy's identification with an angry adolescent in the patient, which was concealed by the compliant and sweet persona. Wendy also became clearer that what she could tolerate no longer was a feeling of falseness between them. They were, she declared, behaving like two robots; so what, she said, if the patient could walk a bit further each day! What was the point of that? A robot could walk! This patient was wasting her life, still living with her parents, never having a boyfriend, basically doing nothing. We could then see that becoming able to walk out of the house was only the first step; the patient would then have to face the bigger questions of what she was going to do with her life.

Wendy knew that she was in a sense asleep, dreaming with her patient, a dream in which she was a robot – but until working over this material in supervision, she could not wake up and think about the dream. Supervision was a process of waking up. I will mention a related personal experience of my own. Often in work as therapist or as supervisor I find that for a time I might feel sleepy, occasionally even dropping off for a few seconds. The experience of waking up is associated with a sudden grasp of the meaning of what is being communicated.

In a dream, the dreamer usually cannot reflect, but is confined to the given role. The dream cannot be thought about until the dreamer is awake. I can never understand my own dreams until later in the day when I am fully awake. Similarly, in the session with the patient, it is often difficult to understand what is happening, what is being dreamt. The dream that patient and therapist are having together is brought to supervision; maybe then therapist and supervisor have a dream together. At some point somebody wakes up and understands what is going on. The experienced psychotherapist may be able to wake up sooner – but first it is necessary to dream, then to enter the patient's dream. Waking up means recognizing the role the patient has assigned the therapist in his/her dream.

Further interferences with freedom of thought

I will now give some examples and clues that indicate avoidance of reflective thought in the supervisee.

One indicator of flight from the thinking space might be an intolerance of silence – a discomfort with the kind of meditative silence that I feel is essential. The supervisee may attempt to fill the silence with repetitive talk which contributes no further meaning; the phrase 'as I say . . .', preceding a further repetition of what has already been said, is particularly indicative. Similarly the rapid presentation of diagnostic and psychodynamic formulations, or very structured and ordered accounts of history, indicate a left-brain-dominated, linear mode of thinking. The supervisee needs to be helped to flip into the right-brain mode, to become attuned to what he/she has intuitively registered about the patient.

What interferes with reflective thinking? Predominantly it is anxiety, exacerbated perhaps by the unfamiliarity of this mode of supervision, leading to a wish to appear competent and knowledgeable. Similarly, competitiveness with the supervisor and the related hatred of feeling ignorant make for difficulties in having an experience and learning from the experience. High academic achievement often does not encourage right-brain functioning. Consider, for example, the way in which, when left-brain-dominated philosophers and researchers attempt to address the essentially right-brain processes of psychoanalysis, the latter are often distorted beyond recognition from the point of view of practising clinicians. Moreover, I know that if I have been engaged in some very left-brain, linear, logical activity, I often cannot 'hear' properly the psychoanalytic communications of my patients.

Failures to achieve a space for thinking in supervision are not to be seen as the fault of the supervisee; the space has to be built. In teaching psychoanalytic theory to clinical psychology trainees, I have often found that if I have only a morning or even a day with the students, they cannot relate to what I am saying and the feedback is hostile; if I have longer the teaching is successful. The difference depends, I think, on the extent to which the framework for learning has been built. Similarly, supervision will not work without this framework, or container. What does this container consist of? First, it consists of safety. It is widely recognized that therapy will not work if the patient does not feel safe, basically safe with the therapist. The therapist has to work at identifying and clarifying the patient's anxiety in order to create the experience of safety. Similarly the supervisor has to work at helping the supervisee to feel safe. But safe for what? Safe to speak freely and think freely. The supervisee needs to feel that the supervisor is trustworthy, that he/she is tactful and honest and will not humiliate them. Assumptions about the supervision must be clarified; the task must be made clear. The task is to think and talk freely, reflectively, without censorship, about an experience. I find that the more this can be spelled out, and also modelled by the supervisor, the more free the supervisee feels in working this way and the more productive the supervision. Supervisors need to learn to be supervisors; supervisees need to learn to be supervisees.

There are some simple techniques for helping a supervisee shift into a more free-associative, right-brain mode of thinking; for example, inviting them to talk about their experience of the patient, their feelings in response to the patient's behaviour, etc. Often this in itself will dramatically shift a flat surface discourse into a richly affectively illuminating exploration. With some supervisees it is an ongoing task to counter the tendency to use supervision as a space not for thinking, but for unburdening – in Bion's terms, the use of the mind as an evacuative muscle rather than as an organ for thinking.

One of the main tasks of the supervisor in this mode is to keep the lines of enquiry open, to refrain from and discourage premature closure, or a too easy understanding based on cliché, deriving from emotional and intellectual laziness and also from the anxiety of grappling with the unknown. The supervisor should never appear too certain, but should always be exploring tentative hypotheses and speculation. To this end I often feel it is useful for the supervisor to think aloud, thereby displaying his/her own thought processes. In my own experiences of being supervised in psychotherapy training, the less helpful experiences were with supervisors who seemed very sure of the correctness of their own view so that I felt that something was imposed on me. In the most helpful supervisions I might find it hard to remember any specific idea from the supervisor, but instead, and much more valuable, what was given was an experience of thinking together. A related point is the importance of acknowledging what work the supervisee did in the session with the patient. I can remember, after carefully presenting a detailed account to a supervisor, laboriously written up, the discouraging impact of questions such as 'What did you think was going on in the session?' – a remark which implicitly invalidates whatever understanding the therapist did manifest in the session.

Example: the thought police

Sometimes it is important to clarify organizational and managerial functions and boundaries as these impinge on supervision. Unless these are explicitly addressed they may silently interfere with the supervisee's freedom to use the potential space of supervision. For example, a nurse therapist, Deborah, remarked that she was finding supervision less useful recently but was not sure why. She was not able to offer any conscious thoughts that illuminated this. She went on to speak of various aspects of her work, which is in the field of drug misuse; i.e. her clients are involved in illegal activities. She mentioned that in the last week many addicts had stopped attending a drug helpline centre because they had the mistaken impression that the drug worker had 'grassed' on them; there had been police raids following a conversation with this worker; purely coincidentally, Deborah thought. Later, in the same supervision session, she referred to the somewhat paranoid atmosphere of the department in which we both worked, remarking 'You don't know who you can trust'. I commented that perhaps Deborah had become anxious recently about the fate of what she had told me, that perhaps she was at this point not sure that she could trust me, and that maybe she feared that I would 'grass' to her manager about her. Her manner lightened in response to this. She said she thought this was correct although she had not been aware of this anxiety consciously.

Groups and the supervisory space

All the points I have made so far can also apply in supervision in groups. Here again, competitiveness can have a markedly negative effect on the supervisory thinking space. Thinking that is motivated by competitiveness is not thinking that is aimed at understanding the patient – although it may masquerade as such. Much responsibility for the culture of the supervision group rests with the personality and activity of the supervisor. Narcissistic features of a supervisor such as a strong need to be admired and have his/her views mirrored by the group tend to restrict the thinking space of the group. On the other hand, the tendency towards a culture of competitiveness can be reduced by the supervisor making something of every participant's comments. This is not just a matter of tact, but rests upon the recognition that different people are responsive to different aspects of the patient and of the interaction with the patient. Because of this, a group is potentially capable of a higher level of synthesis of aspects of the patient than may be possible in a supervisory dyad. On the other hand, groups are more prone to regression to primitive modes of functioning; the group must be encouraged to reflect upon itself in order to counter this.

A vivid example of a group on the verge of acting out, as opposed to thinking, is the following. B began presenting her work with X. She described X as likeable. Some way into her initial presentation, she suddenly stopped and with great anxiety declared that she could go no further because she realized another member of the group, A, may in the past have known X. A immediately offered to leave and B agreed that she should do so. Fortunately other members of the group managed to rescue some thinking space and A remained. Later in the discussion we were able to understand how the pressure for A to leave reflected a collusion between patient and therapist to expel aspects of the patient which were not 'likeable'.

'Raw and cooked' emotional material

In this account of the issues in supervision I have been emphasizing the associative, mulling-over kind of thinking which I feel is an important component. It is not the only component; there are many approaches to supervision. Both brain hemispheres are required; right and left functioning must communicate and work together. In a paper entitled 'Imagery, raw and cooked. A hemispheric recipe', Bakan (1980) describes how the right hemisphere's activity is apparent in sleep, dreams and free association, its mode of operation following the Freudian primary process. When the hemispheres are in good communication, there may be processing or 'cooking' of the raw material of the right brain by the left brain. The raw food and the cooking are both essential. The analytic activity of the left brain must be brought to bear upon the raw emotional material, closer to the unconscious, produced by the right brain; this is the process of reflective thought. Whether or not this is good neuropsychology I do not know; but it is a good metaphor for one aspect of what goes on in therapy and in supervision.

Conclusion

One function of supervision of psychotherapy is the creation of a space for thinking. This thinking is not linear, logical 'left-brain' cognition, but a kind of free-associative mulling over, perhaps more characteristic of right-hemispheric functioning. Wishes to understand quickly, to appear competent, or to compete with peers or with the supervisor can all interfere with this thinking space. The supervisor must work to understand and counter the potential impediments to the space for thinking.

References

Baars, B. (1988) *A Cognitive Theory of Consciousness*. New York: Cambridge University Press.
Bakan, P. (1980) Imagery, raw and cooked: a hemispheric recipe, in J.E. Shorr, J. Connella, G. Sobel, and P. Robin (eds) *Imagery: Its many dimensions and applications*. New York: Plenum.
Bion, W.R.D. (1967) A theory of thinking, in *Second Thoughts: Selected papers on psychoanalysis*. London: Karnac, 1984.
Edwards, B. (1979) *Drawing on the Right Side of the Brain*. Los Angeles: J.P. Tarcher.
Gear, M.C., Hill, M.A. and Liendo, E.L. (1981) *Working Through Narcissism: Treating its sadomasochistic structure*. New York: Aronson.
Grotstein, J. (1981) *Splitting and Projective Identification*. New York: Aronson.
Kohut, H. (1971) *The Analysis of the Self*. New York: International Universities Press.
Kohut, H. (1977) *The Restoration of the Self*. New York: International Universities Press.

Mollon, P. (1989) Anxiety, supervision and a space for thinking. Some narcissistic perils for clinical psychologists in learning psychotherapy. *British Journal of Medical Psychology*, 62: 113–22.

Ornstein, R. (1970) *The Psychology of Consciousness*. New York: Harcourt Brace Jovanovich.

Springer, S.P. and Deutsch, G. (1989) *Left Brain, Right Brain*. New York: W.H. Freeman.

4

SHAME, KNOWLEDGE AND MODES OF ENQUIRY IN SUPERVISION

Alan Lidmila

One of the words most frequently associated with psychotherapy supervision is 'exploration'. This may be understood as a process of discovery, of seeking and possibly finding that which one is either looking for or is revealed unexpectedly. Exploration implies a journey, and fictional accounts of exploration utilize the narrative device of the simultaneous inner journey in themes that deal with soul searching or self-discovery. In supervision, we also understand that within the outward journey, or 'content' of the session there is a journey *inwards*. We are not so much interested in the landscape, what the client is reported to have said, as in what lies within, behind or before: we are interested in the less apparent domain of the subjective and inter-subjective. Literature abounds with many pairings, analogous to a supervisor–supervisee dyad, involved in an existential or metaphysical voyage of discovery: *Robinson Crusoe*, *Moby Dick*, *Don Quixote* and *Heart of Darkness* spring immediately to mind. This chapter examines a few such narrative alternatives in relation to supervision, highlighting some key psychodynamic themes that may underpin modes of enquiry.

It is helpful to think about the question 'What is knowing?' and why it can often be that our response, at least in phantasy, to being known, is one of anxiety, possibly consequently of concealment. Supervision is a project centred on knowing and also being known and it is important to think about how knowledge is signified in this context. That is to say, what it means, and how it is imagined, and how the process of knowing may change from a benign to a persecutory experience.

Forms of knowing

If we consider childhood we have some clues to understanding, for it is in childhood that we find the basis for knowledge and, in turn, a place where curiosity can become perverted (that is to say unhealthy, misplaced or repressed). Childhood phrasings are very important in this respect: 'How d'yer know that then? Who told yer? Do they know?' In these phrasings, knowledge is clearly a thrill and the excitement is based around three aspects: the forbidden, the guilty and possession. Who knows, who wants to know, who shouldn't know, seem to be crucial aspects of the process of knowing as it is transmitted and transacted between the worlds of childhood and adulthood in our culture. As our thinking moves through childhood, the conscious and unconscious conceptualization of knowledge shifts away from something joyous to do with '*communitas*' to something more alien, individualized and *private*. The phrasings then change: 'Who knows more about whom than I do? I'd rather not know, actually! You know better than me'.

The following three examples illustrate how differently knowledge can be formulated:

> I now want to know all things under the sun, and the moon too. For all things are beautiful in themselves, and become more beautiful when known to man: Knowledge is Life With Wings.
> (Khalil Gibran, quoted in Daintith *et al.* 1991: 214)

> I am the very model of a modern Major General
> I've information vegetable, animal and mineral.
> I know the Kings of England, and I quote the fights historical
> From Marathon to Waterloo in order categorical.
> (William S. Gilbert, quoted in Daintith *et al.* 1991: 214)

> [And God told them] ... not to eat of the tree of knowledge of good and evil ... [if they eat] ... your eyes shall be open, and ye shall be as gods, knowing good and evil ... [and woman saw that the tree was good] ... and a tree to be desired to make one wise ... and they did eat ... and saw that they were naked ... and made themselves aprons; [then they heard the voice of God] ... and Adam and Eve hid themselves from the presence ... [and God said: where art thou?] [and Adam said:] ... I heard thy voice ... and I was afraid, because I was naked, and I hid myself.
> (Genesis 2–3)

I will return to the Gibran quote later.

The Gilbert and Sullivan lines caricature a defensive reaction to a problematical 'not knowing': an obsessionally controlling, omnipotent response to a perceived, or phantasized, shaming relation. This form of defensive knowing ('the facts, I must have the facts') can become a property of the supervisory dyad ('I must have all the facts to give, then he/she will know, and then I will too'). It is as if we assume that knowing equals good or safe, and unknowing equals bad or unsafe. This relation carries some relief ('one of us must know, phew!') and, of course, has a flip side ('one of us doesn't and that's me!'). This flip side of ignorance may be experienced shamefully and so leads to concealment.

The theme of covering up is inherent in a further dimension that is most familiar in the creation myth of Adam and Eve. A creation myth is, of course, centrally concerned with knowledge and the Adam and Eve version is also concerned with the concept of shame or sin, most particularly the shame of knowing the truth, nakedly and innocently, with all its attendant pleasures and fears. The myth also contains all the other familiar and potent themes that may be present in supervision: the forbidden, the exciting but shameful seeking of knowledge, humiliating exposure and defensive concealment. The act of knowing is not an unmitigated pleasure because to know with another is not automatically an event of *jouissance*: a place of play, of pleasure, at the 'edge'. Rather, it can be, and this may be something purely Judaeo-Christian, an act of submission to the knower, expressed as furtive, apologetic fawning. Knowing and ignorance may be negatively associated as a shaming relationship.

In terms of Christian myth we should note that it is as if the supervisor becomes a god that is feared, and revered (or, more clinically, envied, hated but also depended upon and idealized). One of the difficult stages to negotiate in supervision is to a position where innocence and ignorance become revealed, and curiosity and desire may be safely experienced. God is no longer forbidden knowledge and we are no longer ashamed of our (revealed) desire.

Knowledge, curiosity and shame

Barthes reminds us that the hope of catching a glimpse – 'the intermittence of revealed skin' between garments, which excites our desire – is fundamentally an oedipal pleasure to 'denude, to know, to learn the origin and the end' (Barthes 1990: 10). Every narrative is an 'unveiling of the truth'. In order to challenge the dynamics of shame we must, to borrow Barthes's famous phrase, constitute supervision as being concerned with the 'pleasure of the text'. This is more conducive to discovery and knowing because of the absence of a shameful sin which has to be hidden from a supervisory gaze. And this gaze is felt, projectively, as shaming. It is all our childhoods.

Some discussions in supervision take up this issue in suggesting that a supervisor has a need to know and a supervisee has a need to remain silent (Betcher and Zinberg 1988). Although the supervisory dyad is fertile ground for problems associated with knowing, this is by no means a necessary condition of the endeavour. Even notions of privacy and secrecy may be unnecessary conjunctions that are defensively formulated because of alienating notions of desire. What I have in mind are two possible formulations.

Privacy as secretive is a shameful self-relation, defensively experiencing knowledge as a persecutory property of the other, whereby supervision is experienced as violation or even humiliation. Alternatively, privacy may be defined as an object relation whereby desire is a *mutual* property of a containing supervisory space where it is possible to have an altogether more playful understanding of knowing.

I say 'alienating' notion of desire because it seems that the first formulation, sometimes encountered in supervision, casts desire as a property of the other; it is something that the supervisor *has*, which the supervisee passively, reluctantly submits to. The look that may shamefully expose inadequacy or ignorance. We would all recognize this in a client–therapist transaction: like the client, the supervisee acts as if their own desire to know is absent, and their own libido (the ability to look) is absent. It is safer for the supervisor to have desire because then it can be resisted, since it has been cast as intrusive. What is feared, and therefore hidden, is both knowledge and also ignorance. To feel someone knows better can evoke difficult feelings that we *should* know better. Furthermore, the supervisee's relation to the supervisor is ambivalent. The 'parental' knowledge is potent but desired and feared; the supplicant position of wanting to know is a comforting infantile need, albeit one charged with envy and ingratitude, with feelings of shame and guilt.

This is an essentially infantile (possibly infantilizing) and, in extreme, paranoid dynamic; it is recognizable as Kleinian terrain. The notion that 'Knowledge is Life with Wings' expresses the onwards and upwards surge or quest that is life or Eros. From infancy the child, according to Klein, is blessed with a drive that is also problematic – what she calls the 'epistemophilic impulse'. Like Freud, Klein's thinking is concerned with what is affirmative and inhibiting in this early questing for understanding via the agency of curiosity which is at first expressed in unconscious phantasy. For Klein (1928) there is a desire, associated with a sexual curiosity, that is about an 'onrush of problems and questions' and an associated, earlier feeling of 'not knowing'. In this sense, investigations or explorations are always riddled and underpinned by unconscious phantasy and all subsequent structured encounters concerned with the process of getting to know more about something are essentially recapitulations of the earliest tableau – a desire to take possession, to get inside the mother's body, so the full facts are both knowable and no longer separate, mysterious, threatening or excluding. The defensive supervisee is reinhabiting an earlier place, where there is anxiety, perhaps hate, for that which is beyond and above us, or not knowable.

Who wants to know what about whom? – intrusion, secrecy and possession

It is worth asking the naive question: 'Whose need to know what?' as far as supervision is concerned. If we ask this question, I would claim that this leads us to a perspective on supervision that is more consistent with an analytic attitude or the attitude that is usually most appropriate for this endeavour. In an earlier paper (Lidmila 1992), I drew attention to an Eastern or Zen 'way of supervision', the contemplative language of which could easily be phrased more clinically in psychodynamic language. When Barthes says: 'The pleasure of the text is that moment when my body pursues its own ideas – for my body does not have the same ideas as I do' (1990: 17) he is, in effect, articulating the practice of free association rather like Coltart's reminder of the virtues of 'bare attention' (1990). This perspective encourages us to reflect with greater detachment and to ask, in terms of the supervisor's 'need to know', *whether* there is anything to know and *what* it might be? This can be distinguished from a *wanting* to know, which is a misplaced curiosity.

Surely the supervisee is the one in whom desire should be located? Needing to know can be an anxious motive, and this in turn will be transmitted to, or collude with any anxiety in the supervisee, with defensive concealment a possible consequence. There is less room for shame if we try and confine ourselves to questions of what we are aware of, which is more along the lines of the mother/child relation where knowledge is something that is explored through a mutual gazing and rêverie. After all, our nakedness, our revealed ignorance or uncertainty are not inherently shameful and, as in childhood, only become so in supervision if there is a *phantasy* of shaming with consequent defensiveness *embedded* in the setting.

A shaming relation only occurs in terms of unconscious phantasy if desire is split off, and denied ('I don't know', 'I won't tell') and then projected as a need of the other to know. The other then becomes constituted as a persecutory super-ego that has to be further defended against and is at the same time identified with shaming. As Mollon reminds us, in addition to shame being understandable in terms of 'the look' and distortions of maternal mirroring, many individuals with particular difficulties around shame experienced their mothers as 'highly intrusive and controlling' (Mollon 1993: 46). Intrusiveness is also a sense of shame and curiosity that is essentially oedipal, the desire to know about that from which one is excluded.

The oedipal triangle is, of course, a break-point, a rupture of knowledge where one, crudely speaking, discovers that there is more to know than one thought. This is surely connected to the dynamic of shame as related to supervision and can be stated as follows:

The supervisory pair and the oedipal triangle

- There is always a third party in the triangle. The child (us, the supervisee, sometimes the supervisor) is always outside, excluded from knowing. What is known is secret, and 'other'. The child needs to know, as in the phantasy of witnessing, and being curious about, the relation of the parental pair. But the child is also afraid of knowing, and so excitement is suppressed, or projected, and the child may want protection from their desire for knowledge.
- The pair may be the client–therapist, or even client–supervisor, as well as the possibility of the supervisor–supervisee in relation to the client as third party. The supervisory task always involves some *revelation* of a third hidden part, or an *inclusion* of the desire of the third. Symbolically, this is a

resolution through identifications, e.g. supervisor with client, supervisee with supervisor. The primal scene may be seen as the client–therapist event, off-stage.
- The third always facilitates a pair, brings them together (the client brings together the supervisee and supervisor as the supervisor brings together the supervisee and client, at least in thought, to help them to work better).

These oedipal configurations find final expression in a Winnicottian nursing triad, symbolized as supervision. The shadow to this is found in ambivalence as when, for example, there is reluctance to bring clear material, a need to remain silent. Here, there is a defensive sense of intrusion into the privacy of the nursing couple as if the client and supervisee have a special relationship. Alternatively, the supervisory gaze threatens because of a concealed guilt about a client–supervisee *amour-fou* or crazy love ('what we did together', 'the sin' of errors and collusions in therapy). Here the triangle shifts and it is as if the supervisor becomes the enquiring child to the secretive pair: a peeker through the bedroom door.

The complex dynamic relations of knowledge that can underpin supervision are likely to determine the choice, conscious or otherwise, of the dominant mode of enquiry and so it is to this aspect that we now turn our attention.

Modes of enquiry

In terms of the supervisory discourse, there are narrative choices available as to how we supervise (or, formalize our desire into modes of enquiry). Thinking in terms of language, how do we attempt to extricate ourselves from a 'rivalry of naming' (Barthes 1990: 30)? How can we, in supervising, inhabit a neutral, reflexive text, one that does not, through its naming, bring forth shamed transferences? As well as the exploratory mode of enquiry, let us consider some other modes, all of which find their way into supervisory practice: the detective, the inquisitorial, the librarian.

The detective

The detective, or 'sleuthing' mode of enquiry, like psychotherapy, is, quintessentially, an introspective pastime, whether it be a personification like Chandler's Marlowe or the intuitive ponderings of Miss Marple (Chandler 1993). Common features abound: typically there is a key figure, the knower, who searches for clues, scrutinizes the text and eventually cracks the case. There is the 'aha' principle of divination, most famously articulated in the phrase, 'Elementary, dear Watson'. In a manner which ranges from the genius to the eccentric, there is also the 'great gifts' principle, a more than sharply demarcated inequality between expert and novice, side-kick or lieutenant. In so far as the penetrative gaze is phallic, the protagonists are either 'cleverdicks' or 'thick-dicks'! This partnership principle may take an alter-ego form that is not a million miles away from the concept of the internal supervisor (Casement 1985). They, therefore, vary from the relatively benign identificatory relation of the pupil to the religious in Eco's *The Name of the Rose* (1992); to the doltish figure of Watson, who marvels at the perspicacity of Sherlock Holmes (which is a good example of a low-key, shaming relation). The private dick is a characterization not dissimilar to Freud's own exploratory introspections, nor indeed was Freud himself unaware of this comparison as has been noted elsewhere (Shepherd 1985; Bollas 1987). When, for example, Freud is explaining the concept of negation, it could be, in a different language, Holmes or Marlowe talking, as all these figures base their investigations upon the slips between the words, the gaffes, mistakes and denials.

> You would not find it at all such a simple matter to deduce from what the patient tells you the experiences he has forgotten and the instinctual impulses he has repressed. He says something to you which at first means as little to you as it does to him . . . [you] look at the material which he delivers to you in obedience to the rule in a quite special way: as though it were ore perhaps, from which its content of precious metal has to be extracted by a particular process . . . you . . . work over many tons of ore which may contain but little valuable material you are in search of.
>
> (Freud 1926: 132)

> What sort of material does he put at our disposal which we can make use of [?] . . . fragments of memories . . . dreams . . . allusions . . . repetitions . . . in actions performed by the patient . . . the relation of transference. It is out of such raw material that we have to put together what we are in search of.
>
> (Freud 1937: 258)

> Suppose you are a detective engaged in the investigation of a murder, do you actually expect to find that the murderer will leave his photograph with name and address on the scene of the crime? Are you not perforce content with slighter and less certain traces of the person you seek?
>
> (Freud 1943: 12)

> There is a very convenient method by which we can sometimes obtain a piece of information we want about unconscious repressed material. 'What', we ask, 'would you consider the most unlikely imaginable thing in that situation?'
>
> (Freud 1925: 437)

> It is my business to know things. Perhaps I have trained myself to see what others overlook.
>
> (Conan Doyle 1993: 24)

It is an old maxim of mine that when you have excluded the impossible, whatever remains, however improbable, must be the truth.

(Conan Doyle 1993: 19)

The latter two statements are Holmesian but we could find similar statements of methodology in Hammett or Chandler (Hammett 1982; Chandler 1993). Freud's own case studies are classic adventures in detection and examples of the text-buster at work in the lonely, heroic figure caught up (in a way that Freud only half-recognized in his own countertransference) in a web of deceit, blind alleys and incomplete clues. Psychotherapists, rather like 'gumshoes', suffer, or perhaps enjoy, an anal preoccupation with dirt, with getting to the bottom of things and much of what we understand as psychotherapeutic technique is a version of playing with discourse, analysing, code-breaking, sign-reading, deconstructing, and, finally, refusing to become a character in someone else's text. In the latter feature, both the therapist and the detective have to become clear that they must *not* fall in love themselves: they must learn to recognize transference love for what it is and for what it is not. Intercutting the genre of film noir with the practice of analytic therapy, it is as if the client stands for the character of femme fatale.

In addition to dirt and love, there are other shared features of these two activities. Psychotherapy, like detective work, is concerned with loneliness, marginality, paranoia, doubt, suspicion, heroism, integrity, independence and compassionate tolerance borne out of an experience of being, necessarily, inured to pain and human folly. These are both unromantic perspectives on the human condition and have to be so in order to fulfil their endeavour. The detective and the psychotherapist share with their client or quarry a sense of loneliness that is fundamentally alienating and is only shared when there is a side-kick or a partner; perhaps this is what is meant by a supervisor in supervision. In terms of technique, the words we may use are variable: 'dispassionate', 'cynical disinterest', or 'objective', 'neutral'. In psychotherapy, or supervision, we learn to trust our countertransference and even use the equivalent word of the detective – the hunch, or intuition. Both figures go from surface to depth or from front to behind, and pay close attention to the fine detail of the text or observable data. Our silent, free-floating attention is as much a stake-out, a waiting for something to happen or someone to arrive at the scene, an activity that requires patience. We are all panning for precious metal and therefore are interested in the grains or trivia of everyday life and speech as much as we expect to find nuggets. We regard a fact as a fact when it is proven and we even share some sense of an enemy, be it the criminal mind or the neurotic id or false self. Fundamentally, we are less concerned morally or even clinically with the deed but find the motive much more important.

The methodology this mode of enquiry shares with analytic work also involves a displacement of meaning for most of the narrative. The dénouement is often a satisfying flourish of the conjurer's cape, a *voilà*! which is the interpretation, the connection, the moment when the text becomes transparent, where things connect. We have solved the crime, or in this context the supervisor has imparted a Holmesian wisdom to the supervisee and this, of course, is mightily relieving because the other feature of these occupations is guilt, a guilt that reverberates through the case and the participants, often conspiring to evoke a sense of guilt in the supervisee. However, in the terms of this discussion, there are clearly problems with this mode of enquiry that lead us inextricably to the dynamics of shame. This feature overlaps with two sub-types, the inquisitorial and the librarian.

The inquisitorial

The inquisitorial model may be more common than we care to think, at least in diluted forms. Consider how much the supervisor questions, or interrogates, rather than merely sits, encouragingly and responsively ('ask no questions and hear no lies'). The supervisee, especially early on in the relationship, may well slip into the role of an innocent, tinged with guilt, confessing error and sin to a paragon of practice. Interestingly, Langs (1979) is keen to emphasize that the supervisor's first responsibility is to the patient and that supervision takes place primarily through an identification with the patient and only secondarily with the therapist. Such an orientation will act to reinforce in a supervisee any existing phantasies of persecution because, however supportive the supervisor may intend to be, a supervisee (depending on personal pathology and status) will inevitably be inclined to think that the supervisor is 'not on their side', 'unsupportive', 'critical' and 'certainly knows something they don't'. Considerable maturity is required of a supervisee to accept an empathy that bypasses *them* and is instead communicated to a third party: unfortunately this may evoke insecure feelings that are likely to be associated with shame and envy.

The inquisitorial model is asymmetrical and inherently persecutory but it may get at the truth. We should also remember that anxiety in the supervisor, possibly prompted by the text, may motivate too inquisitorial an approach, and we should not be surprised to find supervision portrayed as inquisition: after all, it does go on in secret, behind closed doors, at an appointed hour! There are many examples available that show the relative efficacy of this method in obtaining some sort of version of truth. However, this is usually within a confessional mode which is heavy on features of recantation and, at its subtlest, offers the questioner what the victim thinks is the best answer. Inquisitions often work best by small committee or even a pair (as with the soft guy and the hard guy interrogation). But this is a bureaucratic solution to admissible evidence and is primarily concerned with what we *want* to know, with what we can get them to tell us and whether the information obtained fits in with our vision of the truth. It *would* be a shame if supervision contained very much of this Kafkaesque modality and it is to be hoped that reflexivity in the supervisory process works as an effective antidote to any such tendency.

The librarian

An obsessional quest for data, asking about everything that went on in the session, is also doomed to lifeless sterility. The phenomenon of 'pica' is an abnormal craving to ingest substances, especially dirty ones, which, in its derivation from the magpie-like allusion to omnivorous feeding and hoarding, would be a controlling defence against anxiety and inappropriate in any life-like system of enquiry. The problem with statistical analysis is its deathlike aridity, its delusion that data can be hoarded and, like faeces, be picked over, produced and cleaned up. Like the magpie's jewels in the bird's nest, gobbets of supervisory wisdom are useless if merely taken away and hoarded. As dead pearls of knowledge they have not been inter-subjectively created by the supervisee in their own thinking. Any idealized knowledge that is, in turn, hoarded, bought incrementally and then revered, is a waste of space. The hoarding of knowledge in the thirteenth-century monasteries parodied by Eco (1992), or the librarian who knows all the content but has none of the ideas, are versions of this phenomenon. This acquisitive, omnipotent approach to knowing is less than useful in psychotherapy supervision, except where minutiae provide a genuinely better picture and it is, as in the Gilbert and Sullivan caricature, a defensive modality centred around the possession of knowledge as a form of security.

Conclusion

My purpose in this chapter has been to survey some features of the process of knowing in supervision, especially in relation to the dynamics of shame present in various forms of enquiry. I hope I have shown why exploration is the preferred modality with its emphasis on travelling curiously, without a guide, but with some cartographical principles. This is the most introspective, reflective and arguably the most mature mode but it is also the most *idealized*, and by the same token the most difficult. Both incumbents are highly conditioned to other forms of enquiry and authority that are in some ways not without merits and pleasures. For example, we *do* like to be fed sometimes, especially with a spoon, and we *do* ask policemen when we are lost – we ask anyone! Similarly, detection harnesses our curiosity as well as appealing to our narcissism, and the fact-finding approach of the librarian-researcher engages our obsessional defences in the face of uncertainty. A good supervisor does not make us feel a dope, but some styles of supervision can only have this effect whilst in the same gratifying breath telling us what there is to know (that we were unable to see). Our infantile projective phantasies are fuelled by this tendency and it would be better to find a model that expresses our own sinless desire, that permits truly mature relationships.

Other chapters in this collection examine more fully the notion of exploration in supervision. Briefly, it seems to me that the exploratory mode is typically structured as a mentor, master/novice relationship with varying degrees of symmetry as in Zen or some confessional, spiritual-direction settings. This form, although hard work for the novice, is nonetheless one of partnership or at least might come to be seen as such once the possession of knowledge is demystified. In this more detached position, we find a quality that is more developed than in the detective, which is also given to some introspective meandering. I refer to that which is reflective in the supervisory process, whereby the participants treat themselves as well as their process of enquiry as the subject of enquiry: they are reflective and reflexive, they are self-exploratory. This is accomplished through concepts like parallel-process whereby multiple resonances in relationships are explored in internal and external worlds. Finally, the supervisee brings a desire to know, and the nature of this desire is reflected in a way that may illuminate. It must, however, be acknowledged that to be without memory and desire is no mean achievement, and it is not an absolute state of mind.

Competence in this context is, therefore, confidence; a confidence in both parties to acknowledge, to discover what may be desired and known, without shame when there is uncertainty. A more Eastern, analytic attitude would be a basic foundation to this exploratory mode of enquiry in supervision.

References

Barthes, R. (1990) *The Pleasure of the Text*. London: Blackwell.
Betcher, R.W. and Zinberg, N.E. (1988) Supervision and privacy in psychotherapy training. *American Journal of Psychiatry*, 145(7), July: 796–803.
Bollas, C. (1987) *The Shadow of the Object: Psychoanalysis of the unthought known*. London: Free Association Books.
Casement, P. (1985) *On Learning from the Patient*. London: Tavistock Publications.
Chandler, R. (1993) *Three Novels: The Big Sleep, Farewell My Lovely, The Long Goodbye*. Harmondsworth: Penguin.
Coltart, N. (1990) Attention. *British Journal of Psychotherapy*, 7(2): 164–74.
Conan Doyle, A. (1993) in *The Sherlock Holmes Book of Quotations*. Bath: Robert Frederick.
Daintith, J., Fergusson, R., Stibbs, A., Wright, E. (eds) (1991) *The Bloomsbury Thematic Dictionary of Quotations*. London: Bloomsbury Publishing.
Eco, U. (1992) *The Name of the Rose*. London: Minerva, Reed International Books.
Freud, S. (1925) Negation. *Penguin Freud Library, vol. 11*. Harmondsworth: Penguin, 1985.
Freud, S. (1926) The question of lay analysis, in *The Question of Lay Analysis. Two Short Accounts of Psychoanalysis*. Harmondsworth: Penguin, 1970.
Freud, S. (1937) Constructions in Analysis. *Standard Edition, vol. 23*. London: Hogarth.
Freud, S. (1943) *Introductory Lectures*. London: Allen & Unwin.

Hammett, D. (1982) *Four Great Novels*. London: Macmillan.
Klein, M. (1928) Early stages of the Oedipus complex, in J. Mitchell (ed.) *The Selected Melanie Klein*. Harmondsworth: Penguin, 1986.
Langs, R. (1979) *The Supervisory Experience*. New York: Aronson.
Lidmila, A. (1992) The way of supervision. *Counselling*, 100, May: 97–100.
Mollon, P. (1993) *The Fragile Self*. London: Whurr.
Shepherd, M. (1985) *Sherlock Holmes and the Case of Dr. Freud*. London: Tavistock.

5

HOW THE PATIENT INFORMS THE PROCESS OF SUPERVISION: THE PATIENT AS CATALYST

Jonathan Bradley

Introduction

The main challenge of supervision is how to provide useful insights into the relationship between therapist and patient, which by its very nature is private and exclusive. Wilfred Bion describes this meeting between two personalities at close quarters, between analyst and analysand, as giving rise to disturbance which he called an 'emotional storm'. He says that throughout the process, 'storm-tossed but not shaken, the analyst must go on thinking clearly, from which the more disciplined reaction will build up and the troops will not run away but will begin to stand fast' (Harris 1987: 342). Bion assumes that very often the analyst/therapist will not realize what is happening but says that 'if we stay, do not run away . . . go on observing the patient, after a time a pattern will emerge'. Understandably, in such a fraught situation strong feelings do emerge, and these will be particularly hard to contain when the therapist is finding it difficult to understand what the patient is communicating. In such circumstances it is difficult to follow Bion's advice to 'go on observing' since the pressures to react rather than take a more objective stance are very strong. At such moments it is important for a therapist to be able to rely on some internal capacity to 'rally the troops', to use Bion's battle imagery, in order first to stand firm against the onslaught and then, hopefully, to move forward again therapeutically, by being able to observe new patterns which take account of the new input from the patient.

In my view the most effective role of a supervisor is to facilitate communication between therapist and patient, and to augment the resources available for dealing with crises within the treatment rather than attempt to 'take over command' and conduct the therapy at one remove. There may be times of course when it is important for a supervisor to be involved in executive and management decisions and at other times to be directive within the supervision context. In the normal situation, however, particularly within the context of psychoanalytical supervision, the supervisor will be attempting to represent the views of the patient, particularly those aspects of the contact to which, for one reason or another, the therapist does not seem to be alert. The result of the patient being successfully kept in view by both therapist and supervisor can be felt almost tangibly in the heightened sense of communication between therapist and patient.

Such a process could, in Bion's terms, be described as commensal if not always symbiotic, that is, coexistent if not always mutually beneficial! Nevertheless, the picture of two people struggling on a regular, undramatic basis to keep the patient in view – through a detailed written observation, allied to close attention to the report of the contact, and the general atmosphere generated in the supervision session – will be a familiar one to many therapists and supervisors. This 'ordinary' situation will be reflected on during this chapter and will provide the backcloth to a discussion of other more difficult situations which can arise individually within supervisor and therapist, and between them.[1]

Catalysts and change: psychodynamic implications for therapists and supervisors

In his essay, 'Analysis terminable and interminable (1937: 248) Sigmund Freud describes a key characteristic of the analytic relationship: 'We must not forget that the analytic relationship is based on a love of truth – that is on a recognition of reality and that it precludes any kind of sham or deceit.' Within the context of the essay it seems as if Freud allowed himself to be confronted forcibly by the stark power of the statement he has just made, for he resumes immediately by saying:

> Here let us pause for a moment to assure the analyst that he has our sincere sympathy in the very exacting demands he has to fulfil in carrying out his activities. It almost looks as if analysis were the third of those 'impossible' professions [the other two, in Freud's view, being education and government!] in which one can be sure beforehand of achieving unsatisfactory results.
>
> (1937: 248)

Freud conveys powerfully the special nature of a relationship based on truthful exchange and he also accepts the difficulty of promoting real change. Why should it be so difficult? A broad answer lies in the acceptance that the therapeutic relationship has the development of insight as its main aim (Rosenbluth 1968). Some of the dictionary definitions of 'insight' suggest different ways of viewing it as (1) the power or act of seeing into a situation or into oneself, (2) the act or fact of apprehending the inner nature of things or of seeing intuitively; a clear and immediate understanding.

The implication, therefore, is that insight can be directed outwards towards a situation that is external to the self or directed in an equally penetrative way towards oneself. Freud conveys very clearly the unique difficulty of an enterprise where insight into the state of mind of others needs to be accompanied by an insight into oneself, if it is to be successful. As early as 1914, in 'Remembering, repeating and working through', he points out how the patient repeats and relives past conflicts rather than simply remembers them in terms of the past. Because of the particular way in which events and conflicts surface in the therapy situation, 'repeating' implies conjuring up a piece of real life; and for that reason it cannot always be harmless. He considers it essential therefore to:

> allow the patient time to become more conversant with this resistance with which he has now become acquainted, to work through it, to overcome it by confirming, in defiance of it, the analytic work according to the fundamental rule of analysis. Only when the resistance is at its height can the analyst, working in common with his patient, discover the repressed instinctive impulses which are feeding the resistance; and it is this kind of experience which convinces the patient of the existence and power of such impulses.
>
> (Freud 1914: 155)

I will return briefly to the above passage, particularly the notion that the patient only gains insight into the power of impulses lodged within, through a process of experience and discovery which is very much connected with overcoming resistance to the analytic work itself. Before doing so I will look at the other side of the equation and consider the role of the therapist in this process. In his 1914 paper, Freud admits to being concerned about the lack of toughness of some beginners in psychoanalytic practice. He points out that:

> he had often been asked to advise upon cases in which the doctor complained that he had pointed out his resistance to the patient and that nevertheless no change had set in. Indeed the resistance had become all the stronger and the whole situation was more obscure than ever. The treatment seemed to make no headway. This gloomy foreboding always proved mistaken. The treatment was as a rule progressing most satisfactorily.
>
> (Freud 1914: 248)

Freud returns to the theme of the character of the analyst in 1937, with added urgency. He points out that a number of analysts learn to make use of defensive mechanisms which allow them to divert the implications and demands of analysis from themselves: 'so that they themselves remain as they are and are able to withdraw from the critical and corrective influence of analysis' (1937: 248).

Although Freud's remarks were addressing the (acknowledged) need for a more rigorous training analysis for prospective analysts, his remarks can be thought of as raising important issues relating to transference, countertransference and communication by means of projective identification. Melanie

Klein applied Freud's techniques and insights to work with children by recognizing that the expressive play of children can be thought of and worked with in similar ways to the free associations of adults in therapy. She describes in a very punchy manner what a therapist can ordinarily expect when setting out to work therapeutically with children:

> Many children try to discover the weak spots in their therapist through which they may enter into her mind and life and seek to make liaison with the non-therapist part of her personality. They may try to seduce her into being an idealized parent, a playmate, a teacher or an ally against parents. They may involve her as a source of sexual excitement, or by use of destructive and aggressive behaviour they may aim to force her into the role of a punitive authoritarian figure against whom they can battle.
>
> (Klein 1957: 253)

What a vivid detailing of Bion's phrase 'emotional storm', (quoted earlier)! If there is to be insight within the situation envisaged by Mrs Klein then it will be achieved in a way which leaves its mark on patient and therapist alike.

Earlier (p. 49), I quoted the description given by Freud of the process of 'working through'. It will be remembered that this is, above all, based on experience. Bertrand Russell's important distinction between 'knowledge by acquaintance' and 'knowledge by description' is pertinent here. 'Knowledge by acquaintance' is, as the term implies, knowledge acquired as a result of direct, personalized contact with the object. 'Knowledge by description', however, refers to an acquisition of knowledge where direct experience is missing. Clearly the essentials of the technique of psychoanalysis itself and of supervision within a psychoanalytic context are based on 'knowledge by acquaintance'.

Supervision in terms of the struggle to keep the patient in view

I would like to quote briefly from my own experience of being supervised in my work with a young boy whom I have called Chris who had been sexually abused when 2 years and 6 months old and who, in addition, had suffered traumatic separations from his mother from a very early age. I saw him three times weekly, and after three months' therapy, when he was 5, it became clear that the abuse had had a very serious impact on him, becoming confused in his mind with his earlier painful separations. I found myself plunged into a situation where he would try to re-enact the earlier abuse by trying to assault himself anally and by attacking me physically and emotionally. In a way there was both a victim and an abuser in the room, but I found myself being abused whilst Chris was very much the abuser, in contrast to his actual early experiences when he had most certainly been abused.

Despite it being clear that the abuse itself was being re-enacted symbolically through the use of toys in the therapy sessions, it was also the case that Chris had not spoken at all in any direct way about the abuse. In fact I found myself thinking that he would never be able to remember these events consciously and that there would never be a coherent account of what happened. After six months of therapy he came into the room and started to recall through his play what seemed to be an account of the abuse. At the time I wrote the following:

> He came into the room in dreamy fashion. He played with the animals for a while but then lost interest in them. He seemed to lose awareness of my presence and stood facing the wall, leaning against the 'working top'. In dreamlike fashion speaking in an artificially adult voice he said 'keep still little boy, and I will give you something very nice in your bottom.' He wriggled his bottom as he spoke, but there was a smile on his face as if whatever he was reliving at that moment was something pleasurable. But I felt close to tears. It was as if I were experiencing the indignation of being so abused which Chris did not feel at that moment. Certainly the very detailed description of the man involved, including details of his build and facial characteristics whilst seeming realistic, held no sense of pain. Indeed there was pleasure at the recollection that the man used to give him sweets.
>
> Towards the end of the session, however, other feelings about the incident came into the room. At first these were expressed directly at me, as he threatened to hit me and became provocative saying that I wouldn't be able to defend myself if he hit me. Towards the end of the session he started to talk about the man again and said that he shouldn't have done what he did. Finally, at the end of the session, he said that if he saw him he would like to hit him in the face.
>
> (Bradley 1991: 281)

The session I have quoted from and the supervision that followed were memorable in several ways. In the first place it was possible to write down the main sequence of events that had taken place in the room only by putting feelings about the session into abeyance. As a result I found myself 'getting the facts down' much like somebody summoned to the scene of a major disaster. Secondly, the supervision which I received allowed the sequence of events to come to life again so that I was able to integrate my lifeless written account with some of the feelings that I had been left with.

On the way to the supervision I wondered whether Chris could ever recover from an abuse that would exert an influence by calculated kindness as well as rape. The evidence that he could recover was in fact contained in the session. During supervision, I experienced the tremendous support of someone prepared to be available emotionally as well as with intellectual understanding. This emotional availability (based on knowledge by acquaintance) made it possible to appreciate the significance of the ending of the session, where Chris first expressed anger to me and then to 'the man'. It was the first indication that as well as pleasurable memories, there was anger, and a determination not simply to be a victim, but to confront within himself the impact of the abuse.

Factors which can illuminate or obscure the patient

I would like to consider briefly some of the factors which can ordinarily be thought of as having an influence on therapy itself, before considering their impact on supervision and the supervisee.

Money-Kyrle explores thoroughly those aspects of the contact between therapist and patient which can be broadly thought of as countertransference phenomena. He feels that it is important to ask whether there is a normal or correct attitude to patients. Money-Kyrle feels that whilst there probably is an element of scientific curiosity in the analyst's wish to get to grips with the patient, the main concern for the patient's welfare comes from the fusion of two other basic drives: the reparative and the parental. It is the presence of these two drives which makes it possible to think of therapy as being concerned with knowledge by acquaintance rather than knowledge by definition. Whilst it is clearly important that the analyst should possess theoretical knowledge about the unconscious it is also vital that he/she should have personal acquaintance with its manifestations in his/her own analysis. As far as the therapist is concerned, therefore, the therapy of a patient affords the possibility of reparative satisfaction. In some aspects the patient stands for these areas within the analyst's own unconscious which are still endangered by aggression and still in need of care and reparation:

> A partial motive in being concerned for the patient's well being is that the patient is the representative of a former immature or ill part of himself including his damaged objects, which he can now understand and therefore treat by interpretation of the external world.
> (Money-Kyrle, 1956: 332)

The second main drive is parental in aspect. It is not the case that therapists only look at child aspects of the patient but there is a natural gravitation towards early aspects of the patient's self. It is because the therapist can recognize his early self, which has already been analysed, that he can analyse the patient. Empathy and insight depend on this partial identification.

In the light of his discussion of the therapist's attitude to the patient, Money-Kyrle describes what he refers to as normal countertransference. In this (happy) state the therapist is very much in tune with the patient's needs and in what is a quite rapid process, the patient makes effective use of the setting to communicate current needs through speech (or, where children are concerned, a combination of play and speech). The patient is understood inside by the therapist by introjective identification. After the communication is understood it is put outside again, back towards the patient but in a form sufficiently worked upon to be accepted. Thus the process continues. Undoubtedly this is the general atmosphere within which the client is seen clearly and is helped to acquire insight into a state of mind through a process of knowledge by acquaintance.

Money-Kyrle admits that everyone would be happy if the above scenario should prove to be the norm, but for various reasons it does not. In the first place, therapists are not usually omniscient and sooner or later they fail to understand what is being communicated. Usually these moments of non-understanding will occur around vulnerable aspects of the therapist's own self, those that have not been well understood, and referred to pithily by Mrs Klein as the 'weak spots' of the therapist. There are many factors which contribute to periods of non-understanding, of course. There are many differences between patients who arrive for treatment at different periods of their life and in differing states of mind; there are regular interruptions to ongoing therapy and it is not always possible for patient and therapist to resume the work on ongoing concerns immediately after a break. These are therefore obscuring factors which derive from the setting itself and the psychopathology of the patient.

In addition to the above, there are obscuring factors which belong to the therapist. Much will depend on the therapist's ability to deal with a period of uncertainty and breakdown of understanding. The extent to which a therapist is emotionally disturbed will depend on the severity of his/her own superego. If, at periods of uncertainty, we are able to have a friendly dialogue within ourselves then we will be able to tolerate shortcomings without undue distress. Money-Kyrle does point out that much more severe lack of understanding can occur and the severity and characteristic of this will depend on how the therapist handles his own guilt at the breakdown of communication. There would seem to be a fundamental difference between a therapist who responds to being overburdened, by a breakdown of contact, by becoming almost physically taken over by the patient and visiting the sense of failure on him or herself; and a therapist who defends against such by blaming the patient.

Break-up, breakdown, breakthrough

I will illustrate some of the factors described above by referring to the supervision of a child psychotherapist working with a young boy of 10. I will need to confine my comments to one or two sessions from therapeutic interventions which took place three times weekly over a period of several years, and so I will not be able to describe the overall direction of therapy in other than the broadest terms.

The boy, whom I shall call Derek, had a traumatic infancy and early childhood. As well as physical abuse there were unconfirmed reports of many placements in institutions before finally being 'adopted' by grandparents. He was almost impossible to manage at home and school alike, finding it very difficult to remain for very long in any situation which made emotional demands. He was not sure whether he wanted to be in psychotherapy and for a while was very evasive: frequently running away from the room and engaging, instead, in delinquent activity. Throughout this very difficult early stage his therapist was able to avoid being drawn away from the central task of therapy even though Derek found it difficult to attend for more than 20 minutes out of 50. Gradually, he became more engaged, even beginning to become involved in play. Paradoxically, the most difficult period of therapy was when Derek seemed to find it easier to remain for 50 minutes in the presence of the therapist. Inevitably, that brought the two of them closer together and very painful issues relating to the very early loss of Derek's relationship to his mother came to prominence. It seemed the search for the right word became the main purpose of therapy. Whatever words were chosen seemed to be wrong, either too direct or, on occasions, not direct enough. As a consequence, it was very difficult for him to engage in dialogue with the therapist.

Very quickly supervision sessions came to focus on the issue of sensitivity: in extreme form this seemed to be an attempt to produce exactly the right interpretation and to present it in such a skilful way that it would slide through defences. Undoubtedly, the sense of partnership within supervision began to be threatened as such a series of perfect interpretations proved elusive! Almost as a culmination of this process of disillusionment Derek acted, by knocking a hole in one side of a partition space between rooms. Into this space he dropped toys and little figures of people. They fell such a distance that it was not possible to retrieve them. Eventually the wall had to be repaired, with the objects inside.

This kind of behaviour was quite exceptional and Derek seemed shocked by it. Naturally, it had a major impact on the process of supervision itself. The episode was so dramatic and the violence so sudden that much attention needed to be devoted to this. It was only over time that the attack could be thought of as having a different aspect to it; principally, as an emotionally charged presentation of the communication problem. In fact the picture of toys trapped within the wall presented, dramatically, the frozen internal world of Derek, which was 'so difficult' to communicate with. It seemed to me that the search for the perfect interpretation (carried out in supervision and therapy), one which would find its way through every defence had, in some hard-to-define way, precipitated the outburst. The statement seemed to be that some beginnings in life are so difficult, so traumatic that the feelings are frozen and locked in, located in some apparently inaccessible place. Paradoxically, it was a very effective communication of a state of mind, and led to the freeing of feelings not only within the therapy but in the external world, where he had been trying to function by repressing feelings.

The state of mind of the supervisor

In the light of the above section it is possible, therefore, to highlight some of the factors affecting the state of mind of the supervisor. When the therapy seems to be going well the following general state of mind may well apply:

- As supervisor, we are aware that we have an identification with the patient.
- Although we have not come into contact with the patient directly, we feel that we are in contact through the reports of the supervisee.
- We can tell through the reported activity of the patient that there is a process of constructive ebb and flow between the two of them.
- Our comments can be directed almost entirely to considering issues raised naturally through the contact and we then remain broadly confident that we can rely on the process itself to raise issues.
- At this point, we can feel reassured that the patient is informing the process of supervision through the activity of free association.
- We can begin to rely on the material to take root inside and start to free ourselves from the obligation to provide insight.
- We can rely instead on our own inner objects being informed by the process.
- Although we are not in direct contact with the patient we still feel part of a process based on knowledge by acquaintance.
- The fact that we are operating at one remove from the therapy situation can help us to keep more in touch with the essentials of the contact.

What happens, however, when there is a breakdown of communication of the kind described by Money-Kyrle? Clearly much would depend on the severity of the breakdown but, in essence, the process of supervision would be interfered with by similar processes at work within the therapist. The onset of them would differ according to the severity of the breakdown. I offer some of the possibilities that have occurred to me from time to time as supervisor and some that have happened as supervisee:

- Given that the process of supervision has broken down should I give advice, turn to teaching, or perhaps give some general theoretical advice that may prove to be useful in the future?
- This breakdown was my fault. I do not know enough about the topic. Can I find out more? Can I consult colleagues? Can I afford to become a supervisor who needs to be supervised?
- The reputation of the training establishment is at stake. I need to take over the therapy as best I can, show the trainee how to deal with this kind of problem.

I am sure there are many more questions in similar vein. It seems to me to be normal to have to cope as a supervisor with internal turmoil of this kind even if one manages not to gratify the wishes of this aspect of oneself. It also occurs to me that by being able to tolerate the presence of such a judgemental part of oneself it often is possible to resolve a breakdown of communication more quickly.

Conclusion

Almost inevitably this chapter has looked at difficulties within the therapy relationship and the impact these have on supervision. It is, after all, at such moments that the perceived need for supervision becomes greater. But crises, which can test the quality of the supervision relationship to the full, can be negotiated more promptly if they can be seen within the context of an ongoing relationship, and a trust forged from a regular study of detailed accounts of the therapy process. Ideally, supervision itself will take on many of the characteristics of 'working through' seen by Freud to be so necessary an aspect of psychoanalytical psychotherapy. A joint endeavour of this kind can, and does, enable patterns to emerge within the patient and between patient and therapist and leads to 'insight' of a most memorable kind.

Acknowledgements

My heartfelt thanks to my own supervisors and to those therapists whom I have supervised, who kindly agreed to my being able to reflect on the process of supervision in this chapter.

Notes

1 See Grotstein (1983), Osborne (1994) and Segal (1973) for further reading in the area of child psychoanalysis and for an introduction to the work of Klein and Bion.

References

Bradley, J. (1991) An account of the psychotherapy of a sexually abused boy, in R. Szur and S. Miller (eds) *Psychoanalytic Psychotherapy with Children, Adolescents and Families*. London: Karnac.
Freud, S. (1914) Remembering, repeating and working through. *Standard Edition, vol. 12*. London: Hogarth.
Freud, S. (1937) Analysis terminable and interminable. *Standard Edition, vol. 23*. London: Hogarth.
Grotstein, J.S. (ed.) (1983) *Do I Dare Disturb The Universe? A memorial to W. R. Bion*. London: Karnac.
Harris, M. (1987) Bion's conception of a psycho-analytical attitude, in M. Harris Williams (ed.) *Collected Papers of Martha Harris and Esther Bick*. Strath Tay, Perthshire: Roland Harris Trust (14)/Clunie Press.
Klein, M. (1957) *Envy and Gratitude*. New York: Delta, 1977.
Money-Kyrle, R. (1956) Normal counter-transference and some of its deviations, in D.

Meltzer (ed.) (1978) *The Collected Papers of Roger Money-Kyrle*. Strath Tay, Perthshire: Roland Harris Trust (7)/Clunie Press.

Osborne, E. (ed.) (1994) *Understanding Your Child and the Teenage Years*. London: Rossendale.

Rosenbluth, D. (1968) 'Insight' as an aim of treatment. *Journal of Child Psychotherapy,* 2(2).

Segal, H. (1973) *Introduction to the Work of Melanie Klein*. London: Hogarth.

PART 2

ART, TECHNOLOGY AND FANTASY IN SUPERVISION

The second part of the book, consisting of four distinct chapters, considers ways in which art and technology contribute to or affect the process of supervision, and discusses some of the fantasies and phantasies about both.

6

FANTASY, PLAY AND THE IMAGE IN SUPERVISION

David Maclagan

Introduction: the unconscious determination of fantasy

Fantasy, dreaming and aesthetic reaction are all imaginative responses that have often been treated with suspicion in both philosophy and psychology. They share several overlapping features, which have contributed to this habitual mistrust: their supposedly unreal or make-believe nature, their irrational character, and the fact that they are supposed to be subjective phenomena that tell more about the person experiencing them than about anything else. Much of this suspicion of fantasy was incorporated in the orthodox psychoanalytic model of the psyche, certainly by Freud and even more so in the work of Melanie Klein. Its inferior position was reinforced by its association with the pleasure principle and its role in unconscious wish-fulfilment.

Yet fantasy has not always had these regressive or escapist connotations: in the Romantic model of the psyche, imagination and fantasy have a superior and creative function. True, this is not its only function: Coleridge, for example, distinguishes between this 'primary imagination' and more ordinary, selfish kinds of fancy. In fact, his description of the latter, as operating only with ready-made ingredients and as being governed by the laws of association, differs remarkably little from Freud's.[1]

Between these extremes of the sublime and the banal, there is a danger that the normal, everyday contributions of fantasy may get overlooked or undervalued. 'Fantasy' covers a wide range of imaginative activities, some of which are quite functional (rehearsing, anticipating), whilst others, although apparently fanciful, are potentially useful ways of finding out about ('getting a picture of') ourselves, other people and the world at large. I believe that we can make more use of this kind of fantasy in therapeutic situations. Fantasy does not always have to be translated into its unconscious ingredients; it can speak to us in its own right, and we can learn to handle it, to allow it some degree of play. A therapy that values fantasy in this way will include it in many aspects of its practice, including that of supervision.

First of all, it may be necessary to make clear what I mean by 'fantasy', as opposed to the psychoanalytic understanding of 'phantasy'. The latter refers to deep-seated, unconscious phantasies, of the kind described by Freud:

> With the introduction of the reality principle one species of thought activity was split off; it was kept free from reality-testing and remained subordinated to the pleasure-principle alone. This activity is *phantasying*, which begins in children's play, and later, continued as *day-dreaming*, abandons dependence on real objects.
>
> (Freud 1911: 222)

The relationship of such phantasies to consciousness is so antagonistic that they cannot be brought to the surface and worked on by mere introspection – even though this is what Freud himself did – but have to be excavated by a therapist using analytic techniques.

From a psychoanalytic point of view, other kinds of fantasy – daydreams, rêveries, and even so-called 'free association' – are predominantly seen as garbled or contaminated versions of unconscious phantasy. Whatever useful information can be extracted from them is the result of a critical search for hidden meaning, a kind of cross-examination involving what has been called 'interpretation as exercise of suspicion' (Ricoeur 1970: 32–6); in other words, a refusal to be taken in by their apparent coherence or superficial sense. Fantasy, and the imagination that lies behind it, are here shrunk to a mere shadow of their former status.

Obviously, supervision of a psychotherapy based on this assumption calls for a similar wariness: fantasy is something to be guarded against or seen through, both in the case in question and in the supervisee themselves. Here supervision conjures up its own fantasies, perhaps of a forensic or judicial kind: the detection of a missing clue, the re-examination of previously accepted testimony, or the exposure of a false trail.

Towards a conscious approach to fantasy

I want to put forward a more ordinary definition of fantasy. It is something much closer to consciousness, an accompaniment to our thoughts and feelings, a background presence of which we can choose to be more or less aware. Because it seems like a running commentary that is irrelevant or distracting, many people try to suppress it, and therefore do not consciously notice it: some may go as far as to deny they have such fantasies. There certainly are remarkable differences in both the quality and the quantity of people's fantasy activity.[2] I think this is sometimes a constitutional factor, rather than just a psychological block: there do seem to be people who are 'fantasy blind' the way others are tone-deaf.

At all events, there is a strong case for claiming that fantasy is something much more fundamental to psychic life than its conventional association with daydreaming or fanciful escapism suggests. If we are not conscious of its presence, that does not necessarily mean that it is operating at some deep level of the unconscious. It may also be that we are not aware of it because we have lost touch with it in a more ordinary sense. Indeed, the very sharpness of the distinction inherited from Freud between conscious and unconscious needs to be revised.[3] James Hillman puts it well, when he writes:

> Fantasy-images are both the raw materials and the finished products of psyche, and they are the privileged mode of access to knowledge of soul. Nothing is more primary. Every notion in our minds, each perception of the world and sensation in ourselves must go through a psychic organisation in order to 'happen' at all. Every single feeling or observation occurs as a psychic event by first forming a fantasy-image.
> (Hillman 1975: xi)

Fantasy forms images spontaneously as an intrinsic part of our perception of events; it also leads us to visualize scenes and make up stories about them, and these imaginative accompaniments are not irrelevant or diversionary, but central to psychic life.

From this imaginal perspective the significance of fantasy is discovered not so much through analysing or unmasking it, as through elaboration and by following its lead. In other words, fantasy, whether in individual or group therapy, is treated less as an object of suspicion and more as a resource to be tapped. Like dreaming, fantasizing can be seen as giving an insight into both intrapsychic and interpsychic situations. Taken to its logical conclusion, this means using not only the patient's fantasy, but also that of the therapist.

Here supervision involves more of a sharing, or collaboration not only with fantasy, but in fantasy; in other words, just as this kind of therapy (of which art therapy might be a typical example) depends on a certain capacity to trust fantasy, so does its supervision. And we can also have fantasies about this use of fantasy, in which our relation to it might be more one of collaboration or creativity. Hillman has gone so far as to propose what he calls an 'artist fantasy' of therapy, in which therapist and patient work, as if in a studio, with whatever psychic material is there: this material is not necessarily seen as belonging to either of them, in the sense that it has an autonomous existence that does not depend upon personal histories for being understood (Hillman 1983: 108–9).

The disqualification of fantasy: historical aspects

It is worth looking briefly at how fantasy in therapy came to be so discredited. You might think that Jung, who had a more constructive view of fantasy than Freud, was exempt from the analytic prejudice against it; but this is not quite the case. If we go back to Jung's early[4] distinction between 'passive' and 'active' forms of fantasy, we find that he says that the former are presented as irruptions from the unconscious, made possible by a dissociated mental state, whereas the latter are produced by a 'positive participation of consciousness' (Jung 1921: 98–104). Passive fantasies often have a 'morbid stamp' and require careful handling (what Jung calls 'criticism'); while active fantasies express a 'unified personality' and evoke a more sympathetic 'understanding'. Ordinary (passive) fantasies are subject to the usual psychoanalytic disqualification: their latent content has to be sought out, and a causal or 'reductive' approach adopted towards them, whereby they are connected to the patient's past history. However, there is also another, forward-looking or 'purposive' aspect to fantasy:

> To sum up, we might say that a fantasy needs to be understood both causally and purposively. Causally interpreted, it seems like a symptom of a physiological or personal state, the outcome of antecedent events. Purposively interpreted, it seems like a symbol seeking to characterize a definite goal with the help of the material at hand, or trace out a line of future psychological development.
>
> (Jung 1921: 103)

In later writings, Jung seems to be less concerned with the supposed origin of a fantasy and to shift the distinction between passive and active so that it applies more to the nature of the conscious attitude taken towards it: in particular, he suggests that it be treated like a kind of drama, into which the patient should enter in the form of his 'real' self (as opposed, presumably, to an identification with one of the dramatis personae).

This is, of course, the basis of his technique of 'active imagination'. Although Jung was deeply impressed by Flournoy's ideas about a subliminal creative imagination, and it is to these, rather than Freudian concepts of unconscious phantasy, that he is most faithful, his use of the term 'active imagination' only appears in public in his Tavistock lectures (Jung 1937).[5] Whilst active imagination is clearly a technique for exploring fantasy at a conscious level, Jung considered that it should be reserved for the experienced patient approaching the end of an analysis; so there is still a sense here that fantasy is something tricky and potentially dangerous that should only be colluded with under carefully controlled conditions.

What can we sift out of all this? There is, first of all, what I shall call a 'class structure' of fantasy implicit in Jung's earlier writing: the division between crude, unconsciously determined fantasies and the more sophisticated, 'active' ones, which, because of their closer association with consciousness, are superior in their ethical impact. Then there is the technique to be used in elaborating the fantasy so that it can then be interpreted: this is essentially a dramatic, theatrical translation, in which there is always a monitor or director present. Finally, there is the statement that active fantasy, at least in its more elaborated forms, can only be engaged in by 'professionals' (meaning experienced patients, as well as therapists). It all sounds rather forbidding. Without denying Jung's pioneering role, I would still ask: is this really the only way we can make therapeutic use of fantasy?

Working with fantasy as an ally

As I have suggested, there are models of therapy that are more 'democratic', both in terms of their willingness to accept fantasy at its face value, and in terms of their more immediate methods. And if this is the case with the therapy, it will also be so for its supervision. The first move in this direction is to side-step the 'incriminatory' perspective on fantasy: the invitation for it to take up enough rope to eventually hang itself on some 'unconscious' hook. The view that fantasy is always unconsciously determined is a monotone one: fantasy is a much more variegated creature and needs room to display itself.

Let's look at some of the ways in which fantasy can work, bearing in mind that 'fantasy' is not simply the given material – the dream fragment, the picture, the vignette – but also the fringe or supplement that, whether invited or not, surrounds it. If we take a less adversarial view of the unconscious, and don't look on fantasy as being a vehicle for smuggling forbidden goods, then it becomes possible to consider using fantasy as a way of working on fantasy – to speak to it in its own language, rather than prematurely translating it – just as 'the dream wants a dream'.[6] In other words, to get a clearer grasp of what is going on, we don't need to go *behind* fantasy, in order to analyse it: we can get more information from fantasy itself, through imaginative elaboration.

What sort of roles can fantasy play in this? Fantasy is a way of extending or enlarging the original image. By its very nature, it invites us to 'enter' a scene (is there a figure in the window?) or to engage with its figures (what are they thinking?) or to make narrative elaborations (what is going to happen next?). These are 'first order' moves of fantasy; but there are more excursive moves, that depart further from the original scene (the face is a dummy, the window is a fake), and these are often the ones we find hardest to share, even though they may have already occurred to us.

Fantasy can also pivot on word-play (is the figure at the window 'looking out', or is it 'framed'?). Hillman goes furthest in this, advocating (in working with dream accounts):

> When we shift the dream-words around, letting them play other parts of speech, transformation takes place right in our ears. A dream is transformational because it transforms its own statements through polyvalence of its images. . . . Because the dream's words are not concepts that refer, no dream can be interpretatively translated to other referents. A dream can only be interpretatively re-imagined, as one does with any other poesis.
>
> (Hillman 1978: 175)

There is a question in my mind here, about how far such word-play can be taken and still be called 'fantasy'; nevertheless the distinction between (re-)imagination and interpretation is important.

Fantasy, to use Hillman's terms, 'sticks with the image' and respects its mode of articulation; in other words, both its detail and its style. To translate these into concepts ('the super-ego') or symbols (the 'Wise Old Man') is to lose their specific qualities and the precision of their imaginal focus. However, the question remains: what other kind of work can we do with fantasy, apart from simply expanding on it?

Here the means and ends of therapy interlock. A therapy that, in its concentration on identifying problems, complexes or transference phenomena, chooses to ignore the imaginal, will have little use for fantasy in the sense I have been advocating. Imaginal work with the material of therapy, whether this be life-events, dream-accounts, art-works or events within the session, means de-literalizing them, however actual, dramatic or awful they may be, and seeing them as images or metaphors. Images, as Jung pointed out as early as 1912, when he wrote about fantasy as 'non-directed thinking', do not make rational sense (Jung 1911–12: 17–29). That is, they cannot be read simply as statements or representations; they suggest multiple, and sometimes contradictory, readings.

Yes, fantasy can throw out a lead to latent meanings that are so shocking in their sudden irruption that they could be called 'unconscious' in the traditional sense. It can also work, in a less dramatic way, towards getting more out of what might at first look like a thin seam of material. Some of this 'more' may be seen to connect with life-events that are relevant to the individual; some of it may simply do what I call 'kicking up the dust'. But just because this has no immediate 'fit' doesn't mean that it performs no function: for one thing, it can be a way of getting an image unstuck, of touching (or even tickling) it, and bringing it alive. It is a way of 'handling' the image, so that, while no explicit interpretation is given, its valency (meaning its capacity to form meaningful connections) is increased.

Often we don't know in advance where fantasy will take us, and this can feel quite risky for the therapist, or for the supervisor. How do we know what we might be giving away, particularly since our fantasy may show up some aspect of countertransference? One answer is that the therapist's (or supervisor's) fantasies are subject to just the same cautions as any other countertransference phenomena. Whilst this is true, there is a danger that looking at them solely in these terms will confine their significance within a purely transferential frame. What might sometimes seem out of order from that perspective may have a dramatic and mutative effect on another, less personal level.

Once again, the issue arises of how far fantasy is a purely subjective phenomenon. Certainly there is much evidence to suggest that in a group, fantasies and associations can have a collective function. Techniques have been experimented with that use the 'personal' fantasies of other group members to work on one person's dream (Ullman and Limmer 1989). Gordon Lawrence has developed a similar line in his concept of the 'social dreaming matrix', where a member of a dream-group may dream on behalf of the group. And my own experience in art therapy groups supports this; anyone who has watched the flittering of fantasy around an image in a group knows how it makes connections and sets up resonances in ways for which no single person can claim responsibility. It is, however, usually more difficult for someone to 'let go' of a picture than of a dream.

Fantasy in supervision

I have done no more than indicate some of the ways in which fantasy can be used in a therapeutic setting, and some of these overlap with supervision. But are there specific functions of fantasy in supervision? Through the postponed or second-hand nature of their perspective, supervisors are more dependent on (or, as some would have it, vulnerable to) fantasy than those they supervise: they have to fill in gaps, imagine both sides of the therapy, or picture things they have never witnessed. Rather than seeing this as a weakness, I think it is actually something valuable: the supervisor is situated at a distance from the literal; often they are dealing with the history of a story, the echo of a report. This distance makes fantasy pivotal, with all its advantages and disadvantages. First of all, fantasy creates wisdom after the event: it allows both parties in the supervision to explore what might have been said, what could have been picked up on. Just as a picture in art therapy can look very different some time after the session in which it was made, so looking back at a passage in a particular session can shift it out from under the pressure of the immediate to a place where there is more freedom and room to manoeuvre. It's not just a matter of pointing out what else could have been done or said (which fits all too easily into the 'super-ego' fantasy of supervision), but of allowing the material a breathing-space, in which to expand or deepen.

It also gives a kind of permission for the supervisee's less rational responses to be admitted and find a home. This is not a mere letting-off of steam, though the safety-valve factor is important; it is a valuable source of information. The image or the associative pattern a person or a situation gives rise to doesn't just tell us about how we see them; it makes a more objective contribution. As Guggenbuhl-Craig writes:

> To encounter a person creatively means to weave fantasies around him, to circle around his potential. Various images arise about the person and the potential relationship to him. Such creative fantasies are often quite far removed from so-called reality; they are as unreal, and as true, as fairy tales and myths. They use imaginative images to grasp the reality of the other person.
>
> (1971: 45)

Fantasy can gather in a similar way round actual art-works. For this to work effectively, there must be the space to play with the fantasy, to allow it to make its own suggestions. Sometimes a picture proves remarkably resistant to this play of fantasy; but this, too, may be an important factor to be recognized in supervision.

In psychoanalytic terms, supervision might be said to involve the supervisor's countertransference to the supervisee's own (reported) countertransference. This sounds like a sophisticated game of projective leap-frog. As I have argued, the creative use of fantasy actually points beyond this, to a wider dimension of therapy; nevertheless, even in this confined context it can provide helpful insights. The supervisor's fantasies may confirm those of the supervisee – even if these are unspoken - giving a kind of 'second opinion' support to them. On the other hand, the supervisor may anticipate what subsequently emerges in the supervisee's account of the patient's fantasies; thus showing how this material can be intuitively picked up by fantasy, rather than having to be rationally deduced.

Of course, there are dangers to fantasy: it can exercise its own peculiar seductions or get caught up, narcissistically, in its own web. There is a need for the framework of supervision to include permission for the supervisor, as well as the supervisee, to play, in order to lessen this danger, by acknowledging fantasy as such; but it can never be eliminated completely. Fantasy can also act as a vehicle for surreptitious negative reactions (towards the patient, or even towards the supervisee); and again, it is only possible to guard against this to some extent. Or else fantasy may be subsequently shown to be irrelevant or way off the mark; and here there is need for a degree of tolerance for mistakes – something that the supervisor may (unintentionally) model for the supervisee. But then even the more workmanlike stance of conventional styles of supervision has its shadow side: the supervisor may show an impregnable authority or generate a persecutory perfectionism, or even a contempt for the patient. Perhaps a therapy that adopts an artist fantasy or perspective is more likely to admit its human failings.

Conclusion

I have argued the case for the constructive function of fantasy in therapy (and consequently in supervision) at some length because the influential weight of psychoanalysis that pins it down with unconscious determination is so hard to shift. For all the efforts of Jung and some of his followers to reinstate fantasy and the image as crucial instruments of psychic work, and despite the fact that post-Jungian models of imaginal therapy have been around for 20 or 30 years (e.g. Hillman 1975; Watkins 1976) it still seems to be an uphill struggle.

This struggle affects art therapy in particular, because of its intimate engagement with fantasy and the image, both before and after its making (Maclagan

1995). It is reflected in the real difficulty that art therapists have in finding appropriate supervision. But I believe that there are implications for therapy in general. After citing Freud's response to an interviewer in 1934, that he was 'really by nature an artist', Nor Hall goes on to say: 'The idea that the arts are compelling governors of the course of therapy suggests that we submit our work to a super/vision that is artistic rather than clinically diagnostic' (Hall 1992: 88-9). I believe this is not only true for art therapy, but for any therapy that values the imagination and respects fantasy as its ambassador.

Notes

1 See, for example, Abrams 1977: 168-9.
2 This is a largely unresearched area. Singer (1981, Chapter 3) gives some circumstantial data, but they involve quantitative rather than qualitative aspects. A more interesting model can be found in Hobson's 'formal' analysis of dreams (1990, Part IV).
3 A useful discussion of the ambiguous relation between conscious and unconscious experience is in Brooke 1991: 122-5.
4 The distinction is first made in Jung's 'The transcendent function', written in 1916 but not published until 1957.
5 Sonu Shamdasani's research has shown the links between Jung and a pre-Freudian tradition of subliminal imagination (Shamdasani 1993).
6 Lockhart (1987: 21) tells of dreaming: 'I was leafing through Jung's *Memories, Dreams, Reflections* when a piece of paper fell out. On it, poem-like, was written: "The poem wants a poem/ The dream wants a dream." '

References

Abrams, M.H. (1977) *The Mirror and the Lamp*. Oxford: Oxford University Press.
Brooke, R. (1991) *Jung and Phenomenology*. London: Routledge.
Freud, S. (1911) Formulations on the two principles of mental functioning. *Standard Edition, vol. 12*. London: Hogarth.
Guggenbuhl-Craig, A. (1971) *Power in the Helping Professions*. Dallas, TX: Spring Publications.
Hall, N. (1992) Changing the subject. *Sphinx*, 4: 81-105.
Hillman, J. (1975) *Re-Visioning Psychology*. New York: Harper.
Hillman, J. (1978) Further notes on images. *Spring* : 152-83.
Hillman, J. (1983) *Inter-Views*. New York: Harper.
Hobson, J.A. (1990) *The Dreaming Brain*. Harmondsworth: Penguin.
Jung, C.G. (1911-12) Symbols of transformation. *Collected Works vol. 5*, trans. R.F.C. Hull. London: Routledge & Kegan Paul, 1956.
Jung, C.G. (1921) Definitions. *Collected Works, vol. 6*, trans. R.F.C. Hull. London: Routledge & Kegan Paul, 1971.
Jung, C.G. (1937) *Analytical Psychology*. London: Ark.
Jung, C.G. (1960) The transcendent function. *Collected Works, vol. 8*, trans. R.F.C. Hull. London: Routledge & Kegan Paul.

Lockhart, R. (1987) *Psyche Speaks*. Wilmette, IL: Chiron Publications.
Maclagan, D. (1995) Fantasy and the aesthetic. Have they become the uninvited guests at art therapy's feast? *The Arts in Psychotherapy*, 22: 1–5.
Ricoeur, P. (1970) *Freud and Philosophy*. New Haven, CT: Yale University Press.
Shamdasani, S. (1993) Automatic writing and the discovery of the unconscious. *Spring* (54): 100–32.
Singer, J.L. (1981) *Daydreaming and Fantasy*. Oxford: Oxford University Press.
Ullman, M. and Limmer, C. (1989) *The Variety of Dream Experience*. Wellingborough: Crucible.
Watkins, M. (1976) *Waking Dreams*. New York: Harper.

7

THE IMAGE'S SUPERVISION

John Henzell

Introduction

This chapter deals with issues that arise in the supervision of therapists using methods that lie beyond the usual range of techniques employed in psychotherapy. By the usual range I mean those that are employed by psychotherapists in 'talking therapy', the broad gamut of psychodynamic therapy that encompasses Freudian, post-Freudian, object relations, and Jungian schools. In particular, I will deal with the supervision of therapists who augment conversation with their clientele by encouraging image-making of various kinds. When this happens something quite distinctive takes place in and with the therapeutic exchange. Therapy occurs within an 'inscription' which survives the moment in which it was created, rather than being retained only in the memories of the participants, as is the case with conversation. The therapist's notes, or recall to another such as a supervisor, are reports of absent events. This remains essentially true even when psychotherapy sessions are taped or video-recorded. Such mechanical recordings, though maybe useful, are not the event itself, they are a representation – even, one might say, a misleading representation, as are photographs.[1] A painting, drawing or sculpture made in therapy, however, are part of the very tissue of the session; through them the event itself survives as a material object. Freud was at pains to say that a patient's dreams can never be taken to a psychoanalytic session, only their 'dream reports'. When a pictorial image is made, we no longer rely only on such reports, it is present itself, both during and after its creation, and in the case of its being created in therapy both therapist and client, and in turn maybe others, are privy to its existence.

In what follows, I hope to show how this singular characteristic may affect both therapy and supervision. Because conventional psychodynamic models hold such powerful sway in psychotherapy (as well as in art therapy), as powerful as the privileged position of language itself in our culture, we forget the degree to which the very means we employ in psychotherapeutic work, its actual media, shape the meaning of that work rather than being a mere means to an end. My title is deliberately ambiguous. I refer in a conventional sense to how therapy using images is supervised, images brought to supervision are treated as part of the case-material subjected to the supervisory process. Alternatively, and more radically, because of their expressive power and the manner in which they can embody intention and purpose, images may exercise something of a supervisory effect on supervision itself. First of all, I will approach the question of the image's supervision via that which is supervised – psychotherapy.

Psychotherapy and supervision

When we speak of supervision in psychotherapy we refer, without always realizing it, to a number of interconnected but distinct activities. These are often confused with each other and if we are not clear about their differences fruitless arguments arise. Most, but by no means all, therapists do not mean the term 'supervision' to refer to the management of a subordinate worker in a staff team. What is generally meant is a method that one therapist utilizes to help another therapist deal more effectively with the conceptual and emotional problems raised by the clients and patients of the latter. It is an activity practised within a professional setting and may or may not involve therapists engaged in the same workplace. In this context supervision can take two typical forms. First, informed and confidential advice offered by a more to a less experienced practitioner concerning issues that particular patients present. Supervision concentrates on therapy taking place elsewhere. The supervisor may suggest actual courses of action that the supervised therapist could take in their clinical work, that is, it focuses on the patient or client. Second, the supervisor may adopt a quasi-psychotherapeutic position in relation to the supervisee. Put briefly, the rationale for this is that the best way to help the therapist with their own work is to offer them therapeutic help with the emotional problems raised by it. Here the supervisor involves themselves with the supervisee's countertransference problems in their work via their reflection in the transference within supervision itself. Supervision acts as a mirror for the work. For pragmatic reasons these two methods are often mixed together in supervision; indeed it is the very need to rely on the *ad hoc* and eclectic methods imposed on therapy by the contingencies of work that makes us fuzzy about the principles involved. Hence, on the one hand, supervision and therapy may be confused, an outcome which denies that they exist for different purposes – or, on the other, are too rigidly separated, the effect of which ignores the insights a genuinely reflective method might achieve.

It is also generally accepted that supervision is best undertaken between those whose therapeutic practice and philosophy are broadly similar. While this may apply in the circumscribed domain of psychoanalytic training and practice, and indeed be insisted upon by the professional institutes or societies involved, many therapists' working conditions mean this principle is sometimes more honoured in the breach than strictly observed. This throws an added onus on to both supervisor and therapist. The supervisor must pay careful and imaginative attention to how the therapist actually works, to how their methods may differ, and be prepared to learn about this from them. In turn the therapist must be fussy rather than fuzzy, insisting where possible on appropriate supervision, but also be willing to be independent and resourceful. This applies particularly to therapists whose methods lie outside the ambit of the more conventional talking psychotherapies, for example, art therapists and those working in what I might call the provinces or outer regions of therapy - whether these be methodological, so to speak, or literally geographical. In Britain they often coincide.

The image

Apart from the examples of Jungian psychotherapy and the insights derived from child clients' play developed by Klein and Winnicott, all of which exist in the literature, what can we say about the part the image has to play in the psychotherapies that depend upon it? On the basis of this, what kinds of supervision might be suitable, and what can images suggest that enlarge our understanding of supervision itself? Essentially we are looking at a form of psychotherapy where conversation and images are in partnership, where in fact, talking might actually be about these images. Pictorial works may supplant the accustomed dependence on words as the *modus operandi* of psychotherapy.

This is much more than a hypothetical suggestion. Both therapists' and patients' pictorial work has figured in psychotherapy since the years after the First World War when such a method was initiated by Jung and his associates in Zurich.[2] The practice of art therapy as it has arisen in England stems in considerable part from the work and ideas of the Jungian analyst, Irene Champernowne, who actively encouraged artists to work with her at the therapeutic community she and her husband Gilbert Champernowne created in Devon during the early 1950s.[3] Jung, and the psychology he created, have always stressed the importance of the image. Indeed, in both Jungian analytical psychology, and more recently in James Hillman's post-Jungian school of archetypal psychology in America (1975), the image occupies prime place as the indigenous form in which psyche manifests itself. In contrast, Freudian and post-Freudian models of the mind, including that of Lacan, are essentially linguistic. Jungian psychology and psychotherapy have strongly maintained a particular linkage with the eighteenth- and nineteenth-century German tradition of *Geisteswissenschaften* – literally 'sciences of the spirit'. In both *Geisteswissenschaften* and *Naturwissenschaften* science is taken to be no more than a form of knowledge, as in Kant's *Critiques* of judgement and reason, whereas in the English-speaking world only the latter – natural science – has come to be synonymous with scientific enquiry. In essence, psychoanalysis, both Freud's and Jung's versions, took root in this German-language understanding of knowledge, rather than in the more partial Anglo-American view of science. Furthermore, when psychoanalysis 'emigrated' to Britain and the United States it suffered a double mis-translation. It was taken to be both a natural science and, in order to gain institutional acceptance, adopted the style and often the substance of a medical practice. This in spite of Freud's vehement opposition to the medicalization of psychoanalysis.[4] Ironically, it may be that Jungian psychology, because it has always seemed too mystical to be taken seriously by the academic and medical establishments, has resisted this distortion more by being neglected by them.

When speech is, to any extent, supplanted by images in psychotherapy, the whole relationship between the participants undergoes a shift. I should stress that the images I mean here are actual visual images, not the inner 'images' of the imagination, nor the figurative ones of language. Because the patient's image is a statement,[5] it embodies meaning, intention and subjectivity. Further, it fixes these in an abiding form: it is, to borrow Wittgenstein's (1953) phrase, 'a form of life'. As the image is external to its author, another's meaning may come to appear in it. In this way the image tends to escape the personal horizons of its creator and embody the subjectivity of others who engage with it. No more than the artist does the patient have any copyright on what their work will come to mean to others. Where images are involved in psychotherapy, something like a third party enters the therapeutic space. The dyadic relationship, involved in a conversation between two, merges into a triadic interchange.[6] Think of the phenomenology involved when two people are looking carefully at the same thing or scene. One might say their looking combines in the object of their attention; they see both the object and each other through the object. In a quite radical way what they see becomes a fulcrum for shared meanings. This is even more striking when the object is a picture,[7] intended by one of the two parties present to convey feelings, thoughts and emotions. When it is finished and looked at together it is as if what was the interiority of one has become an external form for both.

Compare this to the interactions involved in a conversation. We listen to the other's words as they unfold one by one in time, never together at once in the form of the sentences and passages that, when completed, will compose the communication they intend us to hear. On either side of the tiny segment of speech which occurs in the present lie spaces of memory and anticipation which form the context surrounding queued-up moments of listening, slices of sound spilling out and disappearing into time. Furthermore, when one speaks, the other can only listen, as simultaneity is impossible in discursive messages; and, whilst it is true a speaker hears their own emerging words, this is an altogether different listening (even acoustically) from that of listening to another's speech. At any present moment, conversation is asymmetrical, in contrast to the equality of looking together at an image.

When psychotherapeutic work makes active use of pictorial images of both these phenomena, a triadic relationship between therapist, patient and picture, and the symmetry of mutual looking, become involved. A third feature is the materiality of the picture which gives it a permanent presence throughout one or several sessions. Whilst memory always runs the risk of expunging what was only said from the record, or distorting it, the image remains as the mute witness and embodiment of an intention.

Embodiment and diagram

A further distinction needs to be made concerning the quality of the pictures used in therapy. These pictures, following Schaverien's discussion, may be 'embodied' or 'diagrammatic' (1992: 83–93). Because they tend to represent the popular idea of how images signify our psychological life, I will discuss diagrammatic pictures first. There are many reasons why this popular view exists, not the least being that it is how psychoanalysts, influenced by Freud, often imagine the matter. According to this, the images of our fantasy are like 'picture puzzles' which disguise the 'real' or 'latent' subject matter of our fantasizing. To understand this inner meaning, the image's 'manifest' surface must be decoded according to reductive rules, rather as we interpret the meaning of a charade or 'rebus'. Deciphered in this way images are really the servants or, in the case of psychopathology, the saboteurs of speech. This is because, with the exception of the Jungian tradition, most psychoanalysis conceptualizes the mind discursively so that the image has a symptomatic role against this background; it is defined as a more primitive function, as the non-discursive negative to the positive and apparently clearer realizations of speech.

Images of this subordinate kind appear in therapy as schematic images made with simple materials which serve as prompts for conversation. Although often said to be 'spontaneously' produced, they are destined, and frequently implicitly intended, to be translated into therapy talk. At the 'analytic' end of the therapeutic spectrum such images may be restated in terms of transference phenomena, the patient's unconscious memories of childhood experience, sexual symbolism, archetypes, or other psychodynamic constructs. They will form part of the narrative form of psychotherapy, and if the therapist is imaginative and skilled, diagrammatic images may also help to 'kick-start' such therapy where this might otherwise have been difficult.

We might say here that a narrative gain is often bought at the cost of the image – and this is the least cost, for other more important losses for our psychological understanding are incurred. At the crudest level, the supposed significances of such schematic images are read off as if from some pictorial dictionary: red equals anger; black depression; firm outlines defensiveness;

loose brushwork emotions; verticals or machines masculinity; valleys; hills or water femininity; and so on. The client may even oblige by labelling parts of the image with the appropriate label. Yet it should be obvious that any finite catalogue of appearances cannot exhaust the full potential of seeing; the ways in which we traverse an image do not adhere to the grammatical rules that govern language. At a more sophisticated level it might be said, like Freud, that the unconscious consists of 'inner speech acts', or, like Lacan, that 'the unconscious is structured like a language'. Yet this lexical version of our psychological experience can only be partially true; the symbolic efficacy of fully realized images lies beyond its scope.

Embodied images are utterly different from diagrammatic images. Because they are created in a material form they should also be distinguished from mental images – including those images conjured up in our consciousness by words. While embodied images may possess a cognitive element and interact with language, they occupy a domain of human experience extending beyond ordinary consciousness. They possess the power to sort, discriminate and combine perceptions from apparently disparate realms of experience with extraordinary speed and force – just because they avoid lexical structures. The essence of the image, particularly the embodied image, is that it directly *presents* rather than indirectly *describes* its concerns. Schaverien says of such images:

> Thus, if the client is not too inhibited with the materials, the mental image may be *transformed* into a pictorial one. This picture is not a *likeness* of the mental image, although it may evoke a similar affect. Rather, it is as if the intensity of the pre-conscious or unconscious mental image is articulated in the pictured forms. This articulation could have no other form, no other mode of expression. Unlike the diagram, which needs the elaboration of the spoken or written word, the embodied image is not immediately amenable to discourse. Its meaning becomes accessible in a way which, at the time, has no correspondence in words. The impact of such an image is in Wittgenstein's (1921) sense, 'ineffable'. Whilst the diagrammatic picture generally stays within known territory, the embodied image transcends what is consciously known.
>
> (1992: 87)

In my remaining remarks it is this embodied sense of the image and its psychological consequences that I shall be referring to.

Image, speech and aesthetics

When the image is present in supervision, it is so in the strong sense that is comparable to how we may say language provides the context for psychotherapy. Whilst this is to make a comparison it also stresses a fundamental difference, not of aim but rather of the scope, capability and direction of therapeutic work. Just as therapy is structured within language so, as I hope I have shown, it may also be ordered by the referential schemes of the image. Indeed, as Jung believed, it is arguable that the schema of the image may even exercise a psychological dominance in spite of Freud's dictum that the unconscious is composed of 'inner speech acts'. At least, we might consider our inner life to be constituted as much of images as of language. How many of us, after all, actually experience (perceptually that is) the act of imagination, memory, or the other forms of myriad life that occur in our heads and bodies, in the form of an audible conversation? Isn't this interior world rather a synaesthesia in which one perceptual mode merges into or is exchanged and fused with others? Psychoanalysis is implicitly correct in assuming that much which is unconscious is a 'privatized' version of our early family life; it is surely incorrect, however, to assert that this is primarily linguistic. What makes the stuff of our experience so strange, intractable and opaque to verbal analysis is that its structure extends beyond any orthodox grammar. To fully grasp its experience as a whole the mind spatializes it, rendering it in the form of visual imagery. The unique gift of vision is to perceive the disparate parts of a complex configuration simultaneously. Hence the resistance of symptoms to our talk and, in part perhaps, the interminable nature of conventional psychoanalytic therapy. The image is isomorphic with our experience because it refers so directly to it while defying any easy paraphrase in words – it must be painstakingly translated. In therapy the image, in the form of drawings, paintings or sculpture, presents us with the explicit challenge to undertake this translation of what may appear ineffable, but which so exemplifies our psychological life. It has always seemed to me that a discussion of this that attempts to separate meanings and appearances presents difficulties – that is, the Kantian supposition that the noumenal underlies the phenomenal. What I am trying to say is that art, and aesthetic experience in general, while not exactly inverting this, does point out the absolute sense in which noumena and phenomena (in psychoanalysis read latent and manifest) are indissolubly fused; each is the reverse of the other's coin.

In supervision, also, the image confronts us with this subtle problem, which is also one of the greatest mysteries of art. Furthermore, it gives us certain advantages. In the case of a psychotherapy that actively encourages image-making, the picture stemming from the therapist's work and taken to supervision remains in the room as a third party. There is an actual instance of the work being supervised within supervision itself. Furthermore, this instance has been the focus, and possibly the main one, of the supervised work. In a singular fashion the image surmounts the problem of recall, and with it at least some of the problems of distortion and the selectivity of memory in discussing a verbal description of a session within supervision – even more so than an audio- or video-recording. Via their image, something of the patient or client, as well as something of the context in which it was made, actually reappears within the supervision session, not only in its content but particularly within the physical grain or *facture* of the image. This is why two images that possess an apparently similar content may be radically different in their meaning. A picture's meaning is presented in its embodied form rather than only signified in the lexical code of a language.

In so far as we might say the patient's presence assumes a figurative or latent existence in supervision that is exclusively conducted in words (because this presence can only be indirectly described or evoked in these words), then when their picture is taken into supervision this other presence is literally present as well. This establishes two additional ways of understanding meaning within supervision – two further viewpoints. First, the therapist now sees and discusses the patient's image twice-over, first with the patient, now with the supervisor – a tangible part of the session is re-experienced in supervision. Second, through the picture, the supervisor comes into actual contact with the patient of the therapist they are supervising (the author of the work), with the material expression of their sessions together. To manage without this would be like conducting an archaeology on the basis only of a description of a site, rather than having its shards and artefacts available firsthand. So it is that these images play an essential role in certain forms of psychotherapeutic supervision, helping to moderate it, and, perhaps more than this, exercise something of a supervisory function themselves.

Finally, it is arguable that the criteria that distinguish the truth of a psychotherapy practice, as well as its supervision, are not scientific as we popularly understand that word, nor medical, but rather aesthetic. That is, psychotherapy should be assimilated to the forms of human understanding exemplified in the arts rather than those of a clinical science. If this is so, images and pictures of all kinds must find their place. The mind, and in therapy the mind in distress and confusion with itself, must be, as James Hillman (1975) says, envisioned as a kind of total theatre rather than thought of too narrowly as a logical system. But this is to run foul of the prejudice that casts art as an 'entertainment' in our culture, and science as 'realistic'. For a wide range of psychotherapies, appropriate to the many varieties of human experience, to attain their proper place in society this prejudice needs to be forcefully dispelled.

Notes

1 One of our current cultural assumptions is to regard photographic and other recorded versions of events as the truth. This unexamined assumption is the background to the often propagandist use of these techniques in the media.
2 During the 1980s Michael Edwards, an eminent art therapist and Jungian analyst, carried out historical research into the several thousand pictorial works made by patients of Jung and colleagues at the C.G. Jung Institute in Zurich. This work is unpublished.
3 See Anthony Stevens, *Withymead: A Jungian Community for Healing Arts* (1986).
4 See Freud's *'The question of lay analysis'* (1926).

5 We can see here how difficult it is to find words that describe the symbolic nature of human action without having recourse to the language of language itself; this is why language is so privileged and images so neglected in philosophy.
6 A closely related position to this is adopted by the psychotherapist and art therapist Joy Schaverien (1992) in her *The Revealing Image: Analytical Art Psychotherapy in Theory and Practice*. This is one of the most philosophically astute treatments of images in psychotherapy to have appeared.
7 By 'picture' I mean pictorial image generally, not just paintings or drawings but sculptures or images made with any kind of material.

References

Freud, S. (1926) The question of lay analysis. *Standard Edition, vol. 20*. London: Hogarth.
Hillman, J. (1975) *Re-Visioning Psychology*. New York: Harper Colophon Books.
Schaverien, J. (1992) *The Revealing Image: Analytical art psychotherapy in theory and practice*. London: Routledge.
Stevens, A. (1986) *Withymead: A Jungian community for healing arts*. London: Coventure/Element Books.
Wittgenstein, L. (1922) *Tractactus Logico-Philosophicus*. Trans. C.K. Ogden. London: Routledge & Kegan Paul.
Wittgenstein, L. (1953) *Philosophical Investigations*, trans. by G.E.M. Anscombe. Oxford: Basil Blackwell.

8

THE USE OF AUDIOTAPES IN SUPERVISION OF PSYCHOTHERAPY

Mark Aveline

Introduction

The use of audio- and videotape recordings in supervision of dynamic psychotherapy is controversial. However, recordings give direct, factually correct access to the therapy session which cannot be matched by the common, indirect method in supervision of recollection. Whilst there are arguments against taping, tapes are an essential aid in supervision. They facilitate close examination of process and technique.

Why using recordings is controversial

Supervision is a cardinal element in training. Traditionally in supervision of psychodynamic psychotherapy, the supervisee gives a recollected and impressionistic account of what happened in the session. In contrast to practice in cognitive-behavioural and family psychotherapy, audio- or video-recordings which give direct, factually correct access to the therapy session are rarely used. The supervisor responds to the supervisee's free-flowing account with its emphasis on countertransference feelings, evoked fantasies and mental associations by concentrating on one of three foci: (1) the process and content of the patient's concerns and communications; (2) transference and countertransference reactions between patient and therapist; and (3) the supervisee–supervisor relationship as a mirror image of the psychodynamic relationship between patient and therapist (see Doehrman's (1976) account of parallel-process). Clearly, these foci are on a different level from that so overtly provided by a recording, though the difference need not constitute a barrier to their consideration. As an interpersonal psychotherapist, I find tape recordings well suited to the first and second foci.

The use of recordings is anathema to many psychoanalytic psychotherapists.

They object to a way of presenting the work that does not mimic the style of the therapy hour and where the process of recording may be destructive to essential elements in the therapy itself. Supervisors fear that they will be cut off from a vital source of information which, in turn, is central to the analytic method. Thus, the unconscious processes of the patient, their meaning and engagement with the conscious and unconscious processes of the therapist are illuminated by the form in which the sessions are presented. What is not said by the supervisee in his account may be of equal significance to that which is said; omissions tell their own story just as do fantasies, associations and countertransference feelings. It is to these phenomena that the supervisor attends; he listens with the *third ear* (Reik 1949). The justification for the method of indirect recollection is rooted in psychoanalytic technique and theory.

Freud (1912: 111–2) advocated a particular form of listening on the part of the clinician, that of 'evenly-suspended attention in the face of all that one hears . . . he should simply listen and not bother about whether he is keeping anything in mind'. The purpose is to avoid the 'perceptual falsification' which follows from the therapist being selective in which material he attends to; 'in making the selection if he follows his expectations, he is in danger of never finding anything but what he already knows'. Hearing a tape in supervision may – and I emphasize the word may – lead to an overly literal approach. The thrust of this chapter is that that outcome is not inevitable and, furthermore, that there are special benefits in using tapes.

Other reasons why the use of audio- and, for that matter, video-recordings in supervision is controversial have to do with privacy, confidentiality and ethical considerations. Psychotherapists rightly guard the confidences to which they are privy, but also may have an emotional attachment to the idea of absolute privacy, and find comfort in the indirectness of reporting sessions through recollection. Then, despite the fact that process notes are a tangible record of the session and the privacy of the therapy hour is already compromised in the act of offering it for supervision, they may perceive the ideal being destroyed by the recording. They may also feel that their valued position of neutrality is eroded by introducing the recorder into the frame of therapy. Of course, the first task of the therapist is to foster the creation in therapy of a psychologically safe place wherein the patient may explore his difficulties. For some patients, it is unethical to ask permission to record sessions, either because of the detail of their concerns or because their fragility

---

Practice points

Recognize that recording is controversial in psychoanalytic psychotherapy.

Consider how recording may impact on privacy, confidentiality and ethical considerations, and the form of the therapy itself.

as people would be tested to breaking point by being recorded. This is an argument for being selective and sensitive, not an argument of general objection.

Advantages and disadvantages of recordings

The word supervision is derived from the Latin *super*, meaning 'over', and *videre*, 'to see'. In a literal sense, audio- and video-recordings provide a direct, factually correct vision of what transpired in the therapy session. It is this direct access, unfiltered through the therapist's recollections, that is the prime advantage of the recording. The patient and therapist can be heard in action, and seen if videoed, which is a very different matter from those events being reported. The simple exercise of comparing one's notes on a session with a tape-recording dramatically highlights the deficiencies of memory, especially when emotionally-charged and complex issues are emerging and being explored. In recollection, whole segments of interaction are not recorded in memory, the sequence of interactions becomes reordered, key statements by the patient are either misheard or not heard, elements are magnified or diminished, and interpretations take on a wishful perfection.

Bromberg (1984: 35), a declared supporter of the regular use of audiotapes, writes, 'In supervision, the student must be able to scrutinize what he already does. He must have the opportunity to hear his sessions, to hear himself with his patient, in a way that goes beyond what he heard during the sessions as they were in progress.' Just as the one-way screen in the early days of family therapy provided the supporting team with a relatively neutral view on to the session, so do recordings enable the supervisor in a literal sense to hear and the supervisee to hear again his work (Cade and Cornwell 1985). It is particularly valuable for therapists, at all levels of seniority, periodically to review in private tapes of their sessions, a form of professional self-audit (Rioch *et al*. 1976).

As a supervisor, I find that an audio- or video-recording, provided they are of sufficient quality, brings the patient alive and increases my involvement. The Socratic dictum, 'Speak, in order that I may see you', holds. I am stimulated by the way in which words are used, the metaphors deployed and the images evoked. Snatches of interaction often vividly illustrate the central dilemmas of a person's life. Verbal, sub-verbal and non-verbal communication may be addressed. The medium is particularly well placed to identify such phenomena as the patient filling all the space of session with words so as to leave no room for the therapist to say anything for fear that what might be said will disrupt the inner equilibrium; the nervous laugh that as surely indicates that there is an issue of importance at hand as does the bird with trailing wing that the nest is nearby; the therapist whose words of encouragement are belied by his impatient tone or gesture; and the patient whose placatory dependence is shot through with hostility. The recording gives access to another layer of communication and meaning whose significance, once identified, can be explored. This level can certainly be addressed in the reportage of recollection but, without direct access to the session, more turns upon the skill of the supervisee in giving a full account and the sensitivity of the supervisor to these subtle, important nuances of interaction.

Key moments can be played again and again for micro-analysis. What was said? How was it said? What did it mean? How did the supervisee or other members of the supervisory group feel? What is going on? What does this say about the patient's problematic dynamics? In what ways are the relationship difficulties of the patient in their everyday life being played out in the therapy relationship? What might happen next? How might one intervene and why? What actually happened? And so on. . . . Taping facilitates the study of process as well as content. The detail of technical interventions may be scrutinized and alternatives rehearsed. Times of drama, breakthrough, success and failure can be heard as they happened.

A final advantage, though one of chance rather than election, is that the act of recording constitutes a powerful element in the Gestalt of therapy and may become another facet to be understood and worked with. All is grist to the therapeutic mill.

There are several, significant disadvantages to recording. Recording always has an effect on therapy; its meaning needs to be explored (see below, p. 87). It may be abusive to the patient. In the encounter of therapy, the patient is in a weak position, desperately seeking a remedy for his demoralization and loss of mastery, and easily subject to an abuse of power by the therapist (Aveline 1996; Guggenbuhl-Craig 1979).

Voyeuristic and sadistic tendencies in the therapist and supervisor may be acted out in requiring the recording of intimate details which have been given in trust to one person, the therapist, but which will be reviewed in another setting with unknown people who have not been party to the confidence. Patients with a history of childhood sexual or physical abuse may find it hard enough to speak of their experience without the extra stress of being exposed to recording; for some, the experience in therapy may traumatically reverberate with the coercion of childhood. Paranoid patients or those with so little trust that recording is unacceptable to them may be precluded from therapy if taping is rigidly insisted upon. Conversely, exhibitionistic patients may be encouraged in their proclivity.

From the point of view of the therapist, taping, theoretically, may compromise his neutrality. A more cogent objection to taping is that it is oppressive to the therapist. Therapists need to develop their own creative way of doing therapy; they need to make mistakes and struggle to find solutions. A degree of privacy facilitates learning. Certainly, doing therapy is an intensely personal activity and confronts the thoughtful therapist with his strengths and limitations as a person. Playing a tape is nearly always stressful for the therapist and a pattern of collusive avoidance often develops in supervision, the therapist sparing himself exposure and the feared attack of his overcritical super-ego, and the supervisor identifying with the supervisee and being overprotective. How these issues are handled in supervision is a crucial determinant of whether or not the supervisee needs the cloak of privacy in order to develop his skills. Is the recording being used to humiliate the supervisee by highlighting deficiencies or to aid collaborative work between colleagues and potential equals? The same dynamic can operate in supervisions based on recollection.

The argument against taping that it encourages having a focus in supervision, thus interfering with 'evenly-suspended attention', and the wrong focus at that, has already been rehearsed. Attending to micro-episodes in a session may miss the larger dynamic processes that are more important and distract the supervisory pair or group from exploring them. It is held to be more valuable to approach the task of understanding the session on a poetic, intuitive level, rather than that of factual reality. These objections posit an either–or reality in supervision which, if it exists, reflects an elective choice made by the supervisor. All levels need to be considered. Taping is a supervisory aid; it is servant, not master.

The mechanical disadvantages should not be underestimated. Recording equipment is intrusive, takes time to set up and, often, produces tapes with poor quality sound and image. Finding the right moment on the tape is difficult and listening to any more than brief sequences is very time-consuming. The method contributes its own distortions; the impression of anger, for example, may be accentuated. In addition, for the supervisor and supervisory group, it is difficult to listen to intimate moments and distressing experiences

---

Practice points

(a) Advantages

Direct access to what transpired in the therapy session, unfiltered by the therapist's recollections.

Opportunity to address verbal and sub-verbal communication.

May revisit and replay interactions, thus facilitating close examination of process and technique.

(b) Disadvantages

Does affect therapy and may be abusive.

May promote wrong focus and interfere with 'hearing with the third ear'.

Is exposing for the therapist.

Difficult to obtain good quality recordings.

Security and risk to confidentiality.

without having earned the right to hear them through direct work with the patient; it stirs uncomfortable feelings of voyeurism and helplessness. Finally, it is difficult to guarantee the security of tapes.

The use of tapes in supervision

Tapes lend themselves to many purposes. Three are discussed: (1) trainees' tapes in supervision; (2) in assessment of their development as therapists; and (3) supervisors' tapes.

On the Nottingham Psychotherapy Training Courses, all trainee therapists audiotape their sessions; video equipment is available. They write detailed process notes, often informed by listening to the tape. In my supervisions, the therapist gives an overview of the session(s) which prompts discussion and may or may not lead on to tape being played, the latter being a common occurrence. The tape is there to be used flexibly and appropriately. When the tape is used, it may be played from the beginning or from near the end, both being times when dynamic issues may be particularly clear. Alternatively, a special point of interest identified by the trainee (with the tape already correctly positioned), fellow trainees in a group supervision, or the supervisor is played. The choice of moment might be to illustrate what felt like a key interaction, a time when an intervention went well or badly or the therapist felt stuck, or simply to listen with a prior discussion of the dynamics in mind to see what evidence of confirmation or disconfirmation of hypotheses accrues. It is important to give time to playing successful interactions as well as problematic ones. Collegiate learning is promoted if the choice of when to play the tape and which moment is shared amongst all the participants in the supervision.

The chosen moment is played and replayed with fuller hearing on each repetition. It would be unusual to play more than a few minutes or even seconds without some feeling, new thought or association being triggered and leading to discussion. Occasionally, 10 to 15 minutes might be played to hear how the session develops over a longer period and monitor the therapist's way of intervening and sense of timing. Special attention is paid to the process of the relationship, not just to content, and to alteration in tone and rhythm. Times of increased tension often signal the engagement of core conflicts and the opportunity for intervention and dynamic change (Aveline 1988). Attending to the actual use of words and images fosters the evolution of a shared language of meaning between patient and therapist and supervisor. Technique may be examined, as may the significance of the discrepancies between the therapist's report and what is observed on the tape. Micro-analysis as described in the previous section fosters the elaboration of alternative formulations which may be tested by asking the group to make predictions as to what will happen next; the actual sequence may be followed and its consequences charted.

If tapes are kept, they give tangible evidence of the degree of change in patient and therapist over time. Through comparing tapes, trainees may see how their formation as therapists is progressing and identify areas of performance that need further work. Increasingly, the presentation of taped sessions or transcripts is a required element in the assessment of competence for the purpose of either graduation from training or accreditation. This use makes stringent demands for confidentiality and patient consent.

It is highly beneficial for the supervisor to play his or her tapes occasionally for supervision by the supervisees. Not only will the supervisor learn from the experience but any oppressive myth of the supervisor's great superiority in dealing with the issues of therapy will be dispelled, and the trainees will be encouraged to think for themselves and develop their own strengths. A model of openness and willingness to learn is being portrayed. So often in supervision there is a hidden, destructive struggle between supervisor and supervisee to be one-up or avoid being one-down. This dynamic is undermined when the supervisor has the courage to show his or her own work (Rioch 1980). Also, learning is advanced by seeing experienced therapists at work. An illustration can be worth a thousand words; suddenly a whole range of new possibilities is opened up. Seeing how some issue or dilemma is handled provides a model for assimilation if the practice is good and, when less appealing, a point of comparison which prompts the viewer to affirm how and why their practice differs. Psychotherapists, being for the most part practical people, have their attention vividly engaged when material – that dry, dreadful word for what transpires in therapy – is presented.

Practice points

Taping is a supervisory aid; it is servant, not master.

Use tapes flexibly and appropriately after trainee has given an overview from process notes.

Play and replay chosen moments with fuller hearing on each repetition.

May give tangible evidence of the degree of change in patient and therapist over time.

The supervisor may model openness and willingness to learn by occasionally playing his or her tapes.

Finally, viewing a videotape of a supervisory session, either alone or with other supervisors, is an excellent way for the necessary task of the supervisor evaluating his style and performance in supervision (Fleming and Benedek 1966).

The meaning for the patient of being taped

Being taped is never a neutral event for the patient. Its meaning is not fixed, but is often persecutory in tone. Therapy advances as trustworthiness is demonstrated by the therapist, and the patient's trust builds up. The tape-recorder represents a tangible link into the outside world. Though the door into the consulting room is closed, a conduit is open. Confidentiality, so vital an element in therapy, is threatened. For this reason, it is good practice to have as part of the therapy agreement the provision that the patient can have the tape turned off at any moment that he does not want recorded. In practice, this right, once given, is rarely exercised. When tapes are used for supervision, it is important to emphasize to the patient that the recording is for the therapist's benefit in order to advance his understanding and performance.

Just as with a one-way screen, the recorder readily becomes the object of projections: the listeners laugh at what they hear, they make humiliating and derogatory comments, they broadcast abroad the patient's secrets, and, worst of all, the therapist, so seemingly understanding in the session, betrays his true colours by joining in this assault when in possession of the tape and away from the session. These are extreme, common reactions which need to be addressed as they occur. They say much about the patient's inner world.

Some patients find being taped too stressful, at least in the early stages of therapy. Their objection must be respected. Others use being recorded in a defensive way. If only the recorder was not there, then they would work, then they would disclose. This is resistance and, as such, needs to be worked with. Often significant communications will be reserved for when the recorder is not on; there may be a change of tone to a more intimate or less formal way of talking, a confidence given or a hidden anxiety revealed. The same phenomenon happens in non-taped interviews particularly at moments which the patient can construe as being outside the therapy hour. Patients often make significant communications when on the threshold of the consulting room, either on entering at the beginning of the session or, more commonly, on leaving. Their greater freedom to communicate then may be fuelled by the hope that exploration of the message will be avoided.

Being taped may feel abusive to patients whose sense of personal mastery and proper boundaries has been attacked by coercion and abuse of power by powerful figures in that person's formative past. A woman whose father had derided her views and regularly beaten her to try and induce her to submit to his control was unable to refuse being taped for a teaching event. Though inwardly angry, she felt unable to protest for two reasons. First, the request felt like a hurdle that she had to jump lest she be seen to be not trying in therapy and, hence, at risk of being abandoned and thrown out of therapy. Second, to disclose her inner turmoil was to be vulnerable and weak and would, she feared, lay herself open to abuse by the therapist when he sensed the power of his position. Were she to show her anger and so betray her inner self, she would never be able to return. Therefore it was safer to accede and, secretly, be resentful. In the event, this recreation of a conflictual situation of central importance for her had a corrective resolution. Her hesitancy and tight tone of voice told the untold story of her dilemma. As the situation was explored, she exploded with anger over the therapist daring to know what was best for her. Even more important, therapeutically, was that she was able to return the following week and maintain a good relationship with the therapist; she reported feeling liberated in her interactions during the week.

Reactions are not always persecutory. The tape may symbolize the therapist's interest and concern. When a session is not recorded, it may be taken to mean loss of interest, that the patient is boring or beyond help, and that discharge is imminent. One patient felt much more secure when the recorder was on; it abated her fear of being seduced by the therapist; she had the security of being linked to the supervisor through the tape. Another way in which a comforting link can operate is in a clinic where therapists do not do their own assessments. Should it be the case that the supervisor did the entry assessment and this fact is known to the patient, the result can be a reassuring sense of continuity and of not being lost in the organization. Alternatively, that knowledge may accentuate feelings of having been abandoned and rejected by the assessor who, having heard the patient's story, did not personally take them on for therapy.

The patient's progress towards greater maturity may be evidenced in their attitude towards being recorded. A self-preoccupied patient, who had refused taping and who had difficulty in relating to others as whole persons, only noticed after three years of therapy that her therapist had no index finger. In a first show of concern for others, an important maturational stage, she recognized that the lack of the finger would make writing up notes difficult for him and wished that she had agreed to being taped early in therapy. Whatever the meaning, being taped is a significant event in therapy and its meaning needs to be explored. Often when the therapeutic alliance is strong, taping will become a background issue, a feature of the room rather than a feature of the therapy. However the position should be monitored by the therapist as the changing exploration of conflictual themes may propel the recorder centre-stage and require its re-examination.

Practice points

Being taped is never a neutral event for the patient. Always consider its meaning.

Take particular care to preserve confidentiality and avoid being abusive.

Respect (and explore) objections to being taped.

Being taped may be reassuring and even comforting for some.

Confidentiality and ethical issues

Whilst the therapist, in asking the patient for consent to tape, may be merely meeting the requirements of supervision and have the admirable intent of advancing their understanding and performance and, hence, the effectiveness of his work with the patient, for the patient the request may be abusive or the experience of being taped too stressful to be tolerated. The therapist needs to consider carefully the meaning of being taped for the patient and be aware of how easy it is to abuse the power differential that always exists between therapist and patient. The therapist's wish to tape must be tempered by the individual needs of their patient.

Informed written consent is essential. In the trainings in which I am involved, consent is sought by the therapist near the beginning of the first session of therapy. The therapist explains the purpose of taping and how the tapes will be used. Our usual form of written consent is:

Limited Consent Form

I consent to being audio/video taped and I understand that the recording will only be used for the purposes of supervision, teaching and evaluation within the Psychotherapy Unit. I give my consent on the understanding that the recording will be erased once the above purposes have been fulfilled or when my case records are destroyed whichever is the earlier and that I may withdraw the consent at any time and have the tape erased.

Name _____ Signed _____

Date _____

This agreement has been discussed with me by _____

on _____

A copy of the consent is retained by the patient and a copy filed in the case-notes. It is important that the consent is elective and can be withdrawn at any time. If tapes are retained for teaching or research purposes for more than a year, consideration should be given to renewing the consent at appropriate intervals.

Additional consent should be sought if the tapes are to be used for purposes beyond that of Limited Consent. An example would be case presentations outwith the Psychotherapy Department at scientific meetings. The occasion should be described to the patient and an assurance given that a pledge of confidentiality will be given by the participants. In our Extended Consent form, an additional sentence reads:

> I consent for the recording to be used at professional meetings outside the Psychotherapy Unit where the participants have given a pledge of confidentiality.

When presenting the tape at the scientific meeting, the participants must be asked to give the pledge and to withdraw from the meeting if the patient is known to them in a personal capacity. The therapist or presenter should retain control of the tapes and should not allow them to be shown unless he is present. The only exception to this policy is when a teaching tape has been made and the patient(s) has given explicit consent for this exceptional use.

Special care should be taken to keep tapes secure, both physically and in terms of identification. It is not advisable to write the patient's name on the tape as this only advertises the identity of the recordee. Instead, initials or a coded number should be used. Tapes should be wiped clean when no longer required.

> **Practice points**
>
> Informed written consent to being taped is essential.
>
> Routinely ask for limited consent.
>
> Exceptionally ask for extended consent.
>
> Take special care to keep tapes secure, both physically and in terms of identification.
>
> Review and destroy recordings after a period.

Making recordings

Recordings are at their most acceptable to the patient if they are routine and unobtrusive. These principles help the therapist contend with the process of being recorded. From the point of view of the supervisor, high quality recordings are essential and videotape is more interesting and informative than audiotape. Poor quality sound or vision quickly alienates.

For sound recordings, lapel microphones linked to the recorder by lead or radio-wave provide the best quality sound. They are intrusive and have to be fitted and removed before and after each session. An omnidirectional, or two directional microphones placed on a table nearby the therapist and patient come next in order of unobtrusiveness. If a two-channel sound mixer is available, sound levels for each microphone can be adjusted to compensate for loud and quiet voices. A preferable solution is to use directional boom microphones, ideally with a zoom control so as to cut out extraneous sound, mounted on stands and placed on the other side of the room. Tapes should be longer than the anticipated duration of the sessions in order to avoid interrupting the flow of the session by having to turn the tape over; in individual psychotherapy, 60 minutes should be sufficient. A recorder with Dolby noise-reduction and bass and treble controls is advantageous. Audiotapes of group therapy are, by and large, incomprehensible; videotapes are much better. Finding the correct position on the tape during supervision is difficult. For both audio- and videotapes, it is desirable to have equipment with real-time counters and a facility for memory marking the tape either at the time or later.

After consent has been given, it is best to have the tape running before the session begins. Last-minute technical problems are avoided and the intrusive presence of the recorder is minimized. Some therapists time their 45-minute therapy sessions by using a 45-minute audiotape. This has the undesirable effect of shattering whatever stage has been reached at the end of the session when the tape-recorder noisily switches itself off. On a countertransference level, the therapist may be avoiding dealing with the patient's hate over the session ending by displacing responsibility for ending from him/herself onto the machine. It is important to preserve the right of the patient to have the machine turned off at any moment that he/she does not want recorded.

Practice points

Recordings are most acceptable if they are routine and unobtrusive.

Tapes should be longer than the anticipated duration of the session.

Have the tape running before the session begins.

Take special care to keep tapes secure, both physically and in terms of identification.

Preserve the right of the patient to have the machine turned off at any moment that he/she does not want recorded.

Conclusion

Tapes have theoretical and practical disadvantages. However, these are offset by the direct access that tapes give to the therapy session without the distortions of recollection. In supervision, they facilitate the close examination of process and technique. Discrepancies between the recollected account and the record are highlighted, not with the purpose of showing up the deficiencies of the therapist but as phenomena that have meaning and significance. How the therapist deals with transference and emotionally charged issues can be heard and discussed. Tapes are a useful aid in the supervision of psychotherapy, especially its psychodynamic form.

The meaning to the patient of being taped needs to be carefully considered and monitored by the therapist. Taping should be used selectively and sensitively. Careful attention needs to be given to consent, confidentiality and the security of the tapes. These strictures and the importance of dynamic processes apply equally to cognitive-behavioural and family therapy as to dynamic psychotherapy.

References

Aveline, M.O. (1988) The process of being known and the initiation of change, in W. Dryden (ed.) *Key Cases in Psychotherapy*. London: Croom-Helm.

Aveline, M.O. (1996) The training and supervision of individual therapists, in W. Dryden (ed.) *Individual Therapy: A comprehensive handbook*. London: John Wiley and Sons.

Bromberg, P.M. (1984) The third ear, in L. Caligor, P.M. Bromberg and J.D. Meltzer (eds) *Clinical Perspectives on the Supervision of Psychoanalysis and Psychotherapy*. New York: Plenum Press.

Cade, B. and Cornwell, M. (1985) New realities for old. Some uses of teams and one-way screens in therapy, in D. Campbell and R. Draper (eds) *Applications of Systemic Family Therapy: The Milan approach*. London: Grune & Stratton.

Doehrman, M.J.G. (1976) Parallel processes in supervision and psychotherapy. *Bulletin of the Menninger Clinic*, 40(1): 104.

Fleming, J. and Benedek, T. (1966) *Psychoanalytic Supervision: A method of clinical teaching*. New York: International Universities Press.

Freud, S. (1912) Recommendations to physicians practising psychoanalysis. *Standard Edition, vol. 12*. London: Hogarth.

Guggenbuhl-Craig, A. (1979) *Power in the Helping Professions*. Irving, TX: Spring Publications.

Reik, T. (1949) *Listening with the Third Ear*. New York: Farrar and Strauss.

Rioch, M.J. (1980) The dilemmas of supervision in dynamic psychotherapy, in A.K. Hess (ed.) *Psychotherapy Supervision: Theory, Research and Practice*. New York: John Wiley & Sons, Inc.

Rioch, M.J., Coulter, W.R. and Weinberger, D.M. (1976) *Dialogues for Therapists*. San Francisco: Jossey-Bass.

9

INTERPERSONAL PROCESS RECALL IN SUPERVISION

Peter Clarke

Introduction

Norman Kagan began to develop Interpersonal Process Recall (IPR) at Michigan State University in the early 1960s, and subsequently at the University of Houston where he held the post of Distinguished Professor of Education. He continued to teach this method for improving the quality of human interaction until his death in 1994. Over this time he inspired and enjoyed many colleagues; they continue to work with and develop the method. It is difficult to pinpoint the successive stages in such a lifework, but perhaps the most crucial step was taken when he was a young and respectful academic psychologist sitting in while senior colleagues reviewed videotapes of their teaching: he noticed that these people became aware of and commented on a wealth of inner experience which they recalled on seeing the video record but which was scarcely guessed at by the external observer. He also noticed that his respectful curiosity seemed to help them to explore even more deeply the experience of their original performance.

Over the years Kagan and colleagues refined a sensitive and non-invasive method for prompting a person to help them retrieve many of the passing thoughts, hopes, fears, risks, images, feelings, decisions and perceptions that had run through their minds too fast to be dealt with at the time of the original interaction. This method, which they called the inquirer role, forms the centre of their work but they also provided other useful training material.

In what follows, most of the theoretical and practical ideas have been derived from attending workshops led by Kagan between 1990 and 1993 and from the instructor's manual (Kagan 1980).[1] It is not always possible to specify the source of these ideas more precisely. The instructor's manual offers the scripts of training videos, sample handouts for trainees and valuable suggestions about how to use it. The present chapter will focus on the use of the material by psychotherapists, counsellors and their supervisors, although

Kagan and Kagan (1991) report it to be helpful in improving communication over an astonishing range of settings from general physicians to emergency service personnel, airline cockpit crew and army drill sergeants.

IPR in the context of supervision

Although the IPR method is highly structured and might be described as directive, and depends on audio- or video-recordings of the supervisee's sessions, it is far from the managerial/controlling sort of supervision. Nor does it fit the 'supervision as personal therapy' model, although it has clear affinity with a person-centred approach to therapy and education, and might be described as aimed at developing the 'internal supervisor'. It is perhaps a little utopian in that it trusts the basic goodness and strength of the supervisee to be enough to safeguard both client and supervisee. Indeed, Kagan took the optimistic view that improving open communication between people will reduce the fear they experience and the damage they do to each other.

The method aims to reduce the supervisee's fear of instruction and critical attack from the supervisor and it does this by putting the process explicitly in the control of the supervisee, and by encouraging the supervisor to avoid explanation, interpretation and advice. The method relies upon 'discovery learning', so the supervisor in inquirer role aims to keep the supervisee's attention focused on their own inner experience of their earlier transactions with the client as they review a recording of a session. Any conscious person will experience any interaction through images, thoughts and bodily feelings based on memories of previous interactions and anticipations about future outcomes. It is only minimally invasive or controlling simply to prompt the person to scan such experience, when they indicate, by stopping the playback, that they are ready to explore something they have remembered.

Exposition of the method

The first component of the programme in Kagan's (1980) instructor's manual offers exercises on four 'facilitative response modes': 'exploratory', 'listening', 'affective', and 'honest labelling'. This draws attention to the potent effect that subtle changes in phrasing often have on the willingness of someone to talk to us. It also fine-tunes and enlarges the learner's repertory of responses, and helps to develop attitudes likely to encourage open communication. Kagan (1980: 45) stressed the importance of adopting an egalitarian attitude in respecting the other's expertise and responsibility for themselves. He also emphasized the value of focusing attention on feelings about events rather than on the details of external events themselves ('sort of like the music that goes along with the words'; 1980: 56), and particularly on openly acknowledging feelings about the process of the interaction between yourself and the other (1980: 62). This part of the programme may be unnecessary for trainees already skilled in listening but can be useful in establishing the subtlety of open communication and the complexity of inner experience of interactions.

The second component of the programme, which Kagan called affect simulation, encourages the open exploration and verbal labelling of our feelings about a range of challenging interactions, by presenting the trainee with video clips of actors speaking directly to camera in ways likely to stir powerful responses in them. Kagan considered that we each develop strategies to regulate our interactions so as to maintain a comfortable distance from others (1980: 281). Too far away and we feel bored and lonely, too close and we feel frightened of being hurt, hurting, engulfing or being engulfed by the other (1980: 99). He chose the material in the video clips to elicit such feelings. As well as offering the trainee a chance to face 'personal nightmares' and to discover 'interpersonal allergies' (1980: 99) in the safety of training rather than in their professional work, these exercises alert trainees to the richness, immediacy and individuality of their perceptions.

The affect simulation exercises provide evidence, if evidence be needed, that there is a great deal to be 'unpacked' in our immediate experience of others and that it is worthwhile to tease out, find words for and explore the antecedents of those feelings. Thus they may be a useful preparation for what is the core of IPR: training in the recall process and the facilitative inquirer role.

It is central to Kagan's theory that when we interact with others much more goes on than we can deal with consciously at the time (1980: 206). In moments we attribute intentions, assess risks and opportunities and select and reject tactics for managing ourselves and the other. Since time carries us both swiftly on, we have no time to think carefully and insightfully over every move: we have to rely on perceptual skills built up ever since we began to be aware of others. Kagan (1980: 75) quoted Karen Horney (1945), 'We are born small and feelings of smallness persist', and pointed out in his workshops that we are genetically 'hard-wired' to be sensitive to what is going on between ourselves and others and have a long learning history of a specific social environment well before we can use words to negotiate with each other. The very speed, efficiency and automatic nature of our interacting has a momentum of its own that makes it difficult to learn new and possibly more rewarding and less damaging ways of interacting. So it would be an advantage to slow the process down or to remember all the fleeting feelings and rejected tactics that raced through our minds at the speed of thought (so much faster than the speed of the tongue). Yet unaided recall cannot recapture what has been scarcely attended to. As Penny Allen (Personal communication 1995) has pointed out, our appropriate habitual defences are likely to keep some information out of the focus of awareness when we attempt to recount the events of a session: IPR may help to avoid defensive diversions.

Individual recall and the inquirer role

The IPR method invites a person to play a recording (either audio- or video-) of an interaction in which they have taken part and to stop the tape whenever it brings to mind anything that was going on at the time. Once the recaller has chosen to stop the tape they are encouraged to explore the full range of their consciousness of that moment in the past. This is done by someone in the role of inquirer who prompts the recaller to scan thoughts, bodily feelings, images, hopes, fears, alternative actions, and guesses about what was going on in the other's mind. Kagan sets out general principles to guide the inquirer, a rich set of useful questions to help recallers scan their experience both widely and deeply, as well as important warnings about what to avoid (1980: 178, 179, 183–9, 195, 200–7).

There are two fundamental principles: (1) responsibility for stopping and starting the tape and the extent of exploration rests entirely with the recaller; (2) the focus of attention should be kept on recalling the 'there-and-then' and not on elaborating or speculating in the 'here-and-now'. Recallers are to be encouraged and supported to explore as far as they feel ready to go, and to avoid damaging self-confrontation. The inquirer's job is to remain accepting and non-judgemental, however much or little the recaller appears to be learning. If the recaller is encouraged to take responsibility for their own learning they will be likely to continue to use what they do learn when they are no longer answerable to an external supervisor (1980: 195). For this reason the inquirer's responsibility is restricted to being a friendly witness of the recaller's work and to help them remain focused on what was going on in them in the 'there-and-then'.

A recall session should be introduced with a preamble stressing that during the recorded interaction there could not have been time to put into words all the thoughts that went through the recaller's mind (the 'mind works faster than the voice'; 1980: 183), and there may have been decisions not to say some things, and feelings too vague or difficult to express. The purpose of the recall should be described as a chance to mull over the recaller's own experience and behaviour and to discover other possible ways of interacting in the future. The inquirer should also set out the ground rules about control of the tape and their own role as a curious, respectful and non-interfering witness, rather than an instructor.

In the manual, Abigail Harris and Donald Werner (Kagan 1980: 185–9) offer and categorize inquirer leads which are likely to stimulate exploration of affect, cognitions, bodily sensations, images, fantasies, links to previous experiences, expectations, mutual perceptions, risks, hopes, unstated agendas. As well as initial questions, there are also useful follow-up probes which help recallers to consider the impact of what they noticed on the subsequent choices they made and any blocks that stopped them from doing something they wanted to do. Examples follow (1980: 185–8):

- What were you thinking at that time?
- How did that make you feel?
- Were there any physical sensations then?
- Were there any pictures, images, memories flashing through your mind then?
- Did you think the other person knew what you wanted?
- What did you really want to say to them at that moment?
- What prevented you from doing so?
- Any other feelings or thoughts here?

Such questions may draw the recaller's attention to aspects of their experience which they have not yet explored and so help their self-discovery process. It is, however, important to recognize that 'the individual knows better than anyone else the meaning an experience had for him or her' and that the inquirer's role is to help the recaller 'put the underlying story into words so that the story becomes better known to him or her'. The assumption is that aspects of an interaction that are problematic to a person can be worked on more safely with the acceptant attention of another where the outcome of the interaction is already known, and it is reviewed at the distance of a recording and through the taming effect of finding words for it. This method also affords time to reflect and opportunities to hear yourself say things you have hesitated to say before (1980: 203–5).

Kagan (1980: 174) points out that the relationship between inquirer and recaller is often unfamiliar to both: we are generally more used to an instructional relationship between teacher and taught, so care must be taken to hold the recaller in this self-discovery process and not to slip into criticism, evaluation and instruction. This calls for the inquirer to be assertive but non-judgemental (1980: 183). In particular (1980: 202) he warns the inquirer of the need to replace the rewards of skilful instruction and the enjoyable exercise of expertise by finding satisfaction in watching growth and discovery.

Mutual recall

So far this exposition has referred to what Kagan calls individual recall, where one person recalls privately the experience of interacting with one or more others. The manual offers illustrations of psychotherapy training where the therapist and client separately recall their session with different inquirers: it suggests that the client's recall can be recorded and then, with the client's consent, studied by the therapist.

Perhaps more daringly, the manual suggests that both members of the interacting pair might do a mutual recall; here they both review together the tape of their interaction with the help of an inquirer. Each has equal right to stop the tape and talk about what was going on in them at the time. This may feel safer if each has already done an individual recall beforehand with a different inquirer on the same material or an earlier session. Kagan (1980: 299–319) offers an example of a physician and patient reviewing an initial meeting in this way. It reveals a striking increase in openness and liveliness between the initial interview and the mutual recall session. This may support Kagan's assertion that such exercises can reduce interpersonal fears, although Penny Allen (Personal communication 1995) has pointed out that the power relationship between the pair has also been reset towards greater equality by the mutual recall instructions.

The manual also offers illustrations of the extension of this method from two-person interactions to whole groups of mixed status, e.g. a teacher and her class of junior high students reviewing a segment of her teaching together (Kagan 1980: 360–73). The inquirer's role remains the same in such exercises but may be more complex to enact, and opens up the need for different inquirer leads. It may also raise theoretical issues which will be referred to later.

Structure of training

Kagan (1980: 174) stressed the value of form following function in learning in his discussion of the respective virtues of instruction and discovery learning. It may be worth sharing here some of his hints about the structure of training sessions.

Although in his workshops he often asked people to act as inquirer before experiencing recalling, he recommended (1980: 105–7) that trainees should experience the helpfulness of a skilled inquirer as they coped with their first experience of recall before attempting the role themselves. Norman Kagan (personal communication 1992) also suggested that people often got more out of their first recall experience if they used audio-recording, which is more likely to be familiar and perhaps less likely to invite self-confrontation than video-recording.

Contrasts with models of supervision based on other psychotherapeutic traditions

It may be useful to contrast the IPR model with other traditions of supervision and therapy: where does it stand on issues of transference, interpretation, parallel-process, containment, unconditional positive regard, empathy and congruence? Alison McKay (Personal communication 1995) has drawn attention to the differences between managerial and non-managerial (or consultant) supervision with respect to what Procter (1987) called formative, normative and restorative functions. As a self-discovery method, IPR clearly fits in the non-managerial category with an obvious focus on formative (self-educative) functions. Maintenance of standards and the protection of clients is assumed to flow from the reduction of interpersonal fears and clarification of the boundaries between client and supervisee. Restorative functions seem to be served by the friendly witness's non-judgemental acceptance, and the supervisee's own recognition of having survived the intimacy of the earlier interaction and of their growing interpersonal skills.

The relationship between recaller and inquirer is clearly central to the inquiry. A major function of any social role is the regulation of the distribution of power, and the inquirer role explicitly puts the power to explore and to stop exploring in the hands of the recaller, the inquirer only retaining the right to prompt possible areas for exploration and to remain as a witness to the process as far as it is externalized. The recaller's freedom to take up the powers offered is, however, dependent on their other relationships with the inquirer and others whom they perceive to have played similar roles. It is made plain in Kagan's videos that the inquirer does not need to be a senior partner: one example of the process shows a senior staff member recalling with the help of a trainee, and it is claimed to be a virtue of the method that trainees can act as inquirers for each other.

Coming from the person-centred tradition, the method pays great attention to the need for the inquirer to be non-judgemental and acceptant of whatever the recaller says and chooses to explore or ignore; yet it has no place for feeding back reflections or empathic insights or congruent feelings; moreover the nature of the prompting has a directive aspect. The inquirer has to be warm and yet strangely uninvolved; so there is some flavour of the blank screen which might foster transferential processes, both positive and negative. However, there is no place for interpretation of transference on to the inquirer, only queries about whether the material recalled had echoes from other occasions in the 'there-and-then' of the recording. This unusual behaviour of the inquirer may, of course, provide a very valuable 'corrective experience' of non-invasive attention and companionship during exploration of sensitive material. Similarly, the situation of reviewing material in this formal way with a non-judgemental witness and at the distance of a recording may offer valuable containment for the terrors of intimate interaction. The lack of reflection, display of empathy and of congruence may be necessary to counterbalance the directiveness of the prompting, and the inquirer's abstinence from transferential interpretations helps to emphasize the recaller's sovereignty in the exploratory process.

Perhaps a clearer difference between this method and others is its apparent neglect of the concept of parallel-process: the possibility that the interaction between inquirer and recaller is a reflection of the interaction between trainee and client is not addressed. This process of looking at such a possibility seems a precious tradition in psychoanalytic, person-centred and personal construct therapy training. The omission may be remedied to some extent by the IPR tradition of recording an inquiry and then inquiring upon that, rather in the way that conscientious personal construct therapists study their own processes: in this sense IPR is a reflexive method.

Evaluation of the IPR method

It is a fundamental feature of the IPR inquirer role that the inquirer should honour the recaller's sovereignty over the process of exploration of the recorded material and should avoid any invasion or exploitation of the recaller. It is this stance which helps the recaller to feel supported and encourages them to lower their defences, thus fostering their willingness to change to more open ways of communicating. As Kagan has said in his workshops, greater skill in opening communication will not be exercised if the person is uncomfortable with the degree of intimacy which that openness is likely to produce. There seems little doubt that the inquiry method allows the recaller better access to their experience of the interaction being studied, but the effect of this on their willingness to make use of these insights for the benefit of their clients remains a separate question. As in any outcome study of therapy, the philosophy and faith of the evaluator are paramount: this reviewer accepts the assumption that the effects are beneficial but feels that the quality of the relationship between inquirer and recaller and the recaller's experience of such loving and non-invasive support are major determinants of the formative, normative and restorative effects of IPR in supervision. However, earlier experience of less facilitative learning settings may make it difficult for some people to engage in this way of working.

It seems clear that if we are to make use of recordings of therapy sessions the inquiry method is a good way to do it, but it necessarily encounters the practical and ethical issues about first making those recordings. This reviewer refers the reader to the preceding chapter in this book by Mark Aveline and to a recent paper by Horton and Bayne (1994) for discussion of such issues.

Difficulties in enacting the inquirer role

It is also worth considering how far Kagan's method succeeds in achieving its ambitious aim of directing the recaller's attention to the full range of experience of the earlier interaction. The 'inquirer leads' offered cover many aspects of that experience, explicitly drawing attention to the recaller's thoughts and feelings, hopes and fears, intentions, sensory contents and their beliefs about the other person's (simultaneous) experience of themselves, of the recaller and of the physical setting. Nevertheless, there are some gaps and tactical problems. For instance, the manual does not offer inquirer leads over all sensory modalities: for example, although attention is drawn to physical sensations and images or pictures (as distinct from thoughts and maybe words) no suggestions are included about the rich evocativeness of voices, sounds, smells, tastes or touches. There will not be opportunities to cover all of these each time the recaller stops the tape to explore, but over a series of sessions the recaller is likely to learn to scan their experience more widely and thoroughly.

The inquirer has to develop skill in selecting leads appropriate to the moment, for example, deciding whether to ask about aspects the recaller has not spontaneously mentioned or to take the exploration deeper by asking about the impact of those perceptions or their antecedents or the predictions that flow from them. Thus, although the inquirer does not need to be a more experienced therapist than the supervisee, the skill of the inquirer is probably important in shaping the outcome of the recall session. The relationship between inquirer and recaller outside the recall session will also affect the inquirer's tactics and the recaller's responses: a supervisor will probably have a different agenda and different effect compared to a peer or a stranger.

One difficult issue for the inquirer is to decide whether to ask about the 'there-and-then' or the 'before-there-and-then'. The manual offers leads like 'Was that a familiar feeling?' or 'Have you experienced that before?', but it also urges the inquirer to keep the recaller's attention on the recorded interaction and to avoid initiating a new interactive exploration. This might be especially complex for a supervisor inclined to focus on the therapist's countertransference on to the client. A similar difficulty arises in asking about predictions made at the time (appropriate) while discouraging hypothetical 'what-ifs' and 'if-onlys' raised in the 'here-and-now' (inappropriate).

The manual also omits a discussion of the interesting and important effect of the recaller's discovery of aspects of their own or the client's behaviour that they had not been aware of in the 'there-and-then'. This is particularly striking when a video-recording reveals body language at variance with the recalled experience, presumably because it was dissociated in the 'there-and-then'. This is a striking and not uncommon experience but the manual does not offer a framework for tackling the discrepancy. There are warnings (Kagan 1980: 206) that, despite advice to the recaller that the exercise is not about self-confrontation, it will still occur. Indeed, it is unlikely that simple instructions would deter people from attacking themselves if that is their habitual attitude to themselves. It would be helpful if the method offered advice about how to deal with it within the model. The development of a lively, friendly and efficient internal supervisor in contrast to a harsh, critical super-ego is crucial for making therapy safe for all parties. Perhaps it is best to see the inquiry method as offering rich material which then needs to be processed within the theoretical framework that the supervisor and supervisee already work with.

Issues about mutual recall

The mutual recall method raises further theoretical issues. It certainly appears to be a powerful and exciting way of working but it challenges one of the basic principles of IPR, namely that the recaller has sole right to choose when to stop the tape to explore. In this modality, each can be given the right to stop the tape when they want to, but neither has the right to keep it running if they do not want to explore when the other stops it. The suggestion (Kagan 1980: 188) that the inquirer may ask the person who did not stop the tape if they had been aware in the 'there-and-then' of what the other has just shared clearly changes the power balance and may at times be experienced as threatening. The inquirer's agenda may also disturb this power balance even if that agenda is simply to be scrupulously neutral or 'fair' to all recallers. Since the partners in mutual recall often address questions to each other, as well as describing their own recollections, it may become difficult to distinguish between recall of the earlier interaction and a new ongoing 'here-and-now' interaction. In his workshops, Kagan said he handled such a problem by interrupting the recall session and suggesting the inquirer leave the room while the pair continue their interaction in private.

Diana Syder (Personal communication 1995) reported that an inquirer working with two people recalling a group session faces a further complication in keeping the focus on the 'there-and-then' in that the absent group may seem to enter the room as well.

Resources needed

This point leads to what may seem an overwhelming practical handicap of the method, namely that inquiring on an hour's therapy session would need several hours of inquirer/recaller interaction. The objection is not as serious as it seems. Once the discipline of the inquirer role has been internalized, it seems people find themselves using the method to scan their experience when thinking about a wide variety of interactions and not merely when reviewing recorded material (Kagan 1980: 204). Moreover, in the setting of training as opposed to supervision of ongoing practice, a lot of time has to be invested anyway and this method can make highly efficient use of peer-supervision. Also, by reducing the trainee's anxiety about satisfying the requirements of the supervisor, it helps them turn more of their attention to their own learning needs.

On the basis of her own experience, Diana Syder (1995) questioned Kagan's view that a peer or junior makes just as helpful an inquirer as a senior colleague but thought that might be because they might be less skilful in offering the normative and restorative aspects of supervision. Penny Allen (1995) and Diana Syder (1995) have separately evolved a valuable adaptation of the method which relies on Kagan's declaration (in workshops) that inquiring on any segment of a session is likely to throw up the same basic issues. It also offers some answers to the question that often comes up in workshops: 'After the inquiry is over, then what?' When using recorded material they define a period – say 20 minutes – as a recall session during which they strictly enact the inquirer role. When that time is up, they then move into their own supervisory mode, which will vary according to the context. This strategy allows for exploration of parallel-processing issues, therapeutic support and containment, advice or instruction. Such flexibility might not be acceptable in some models of supervision, and certainly calls for a high degree of sensitivity and versatility in the supervisor. This way of using recall with the help of an inquirer for a brief period, to recapture the vividness of the original session and to give time for reflection before moving into other sorts of discussion, may be particularly useful for experienced therapists in long-term supervision.

It is usual when teaching the method to have one video-camera, -recorder and screen for every four participants. However, while video-recordings clearly offer rich cues to stimulate recall and give fuller feedback on body language, simple audio-recording facilities suffice for effective review of conversational interactions. It is also worth noting that recallers are able to work effectively from quite low fidelity recordings.

Conclusion

The IPR method has been evolved over three decades of training and research and has proven useful to many trainers and workers in many fields. It clearly offers a rich way of reviewing recorded interactions for the participants and of facilitating the development of the internal supervisor. Kagan has left us with a valuable heritage which deserves detailed examination and further elaboration. For those who feel it appropriate to make recordings of therapeutic interactions it can be unreservedly recommended as a sensitive method for learning from your own recorded material.

Kagan's original training package is sometimes seen as suffering from its time and culture: material appropriate to the United States in the 1970s can jar on contemporary British eyes and ears and culture. The original film material was put together to maintain the integrity of the method against the inevitable degradation resulting from serial reproduction by many trainers (Norman Kagan, Personal communication 1992) and can serve as a template for producing new material. It is also worth stressing that although audio-visual material is usually used in IPR training and some sort of recording process is needed for the raw material, neither training nor routine use of the recaller and inquirer roles demand more technological resources than a simple audiotape-recorder.

Acknowledgements

The writer gratefully acknowledges the stimulating and helpful discussions he has enjoyed with colleagues in the British IPR Association before and during the preparation of this chapter and wishes to thank Penny Allen, Alison McKay, William Stiles and Diana Syder for their comments on early drafts.

Note

1 Kagan (1980). That edition of the manual is now out of print but much of the material in it is still available on videotape from the Educational Methods Unit of Oxford Brookes University. Henya Kagan (Personal communication 1995) reports that she has completed the revision of the whole IPR package on which she and Norman Kagan were engaged at the time of his death.

References

Horney, K. (1945) *Our Inner Conflicts: A constructive theory of neurosis*. New York: Norton.

Horton, I. and Bayne, R. (1994) Some guidelines on the use of audio-tape recordings in counsellor education and training. *Counselling*, 5: 213–4.

Kagan, N. (1980) *Interpersonal Process Recall: a method of influencing human interaction*. Houston: Mason Media.

Kagan, N. and Kagan, H. (1991) IPR – A research/training model, in P.N. Dowrick and Associates, *Practical Guide to Using Video in the Behavioural Sciences*. New York: John Wiley and Sons.

Procter, B. (1987) Supervision. A cooperative exercise in accountability, in M. Marken and M. Payne (eds) *Enabling and Ensuring*. Leicester: National Youth Bureau.

PART 3

DEVELOPING THE QUALITY OF SUPERVISION

The third part of the book presents three different areas in which quality needs improving, such as supervision within organizations where resources and training are limited; in developing sensitivity to issues of race and culture in supervisors; and finally, in preparing the supervisors for their tasks and role.

10

PEER GROUP SUPERVISION

Jim Gomersall

> There is no such thing as therapy. Only the therapist, the patient and the communications which pass between them.
> (Thomas Szasz 1965)

The need for the peer group

Long before civilization, whilst human beings still hunted and gathered, groups, no doubt, met together to discuss techniques of the chase and the collection and use of the gifts of nature. There is evidence that some cave paintings may have been part of such discussions. Perhaps these were the very first recorded technical guides. With the increasing complexity of our society, the need to meet together to discuss both the nature of the tasks and the cooperation required to achieve them has increased in importance.

There has been a tendency in the helping and caring professions to issue guidelines on the way in which work with clients should be carried out. The precise ordering of cooperative effort is carefully prescribed and the monitoring of outcome accurately audited. Carl Jung has been credited with the aphorism, 'Organize a thing and you will kill it. Don't organize a thing and you will lose it.' Today's professional workers often require support to enable them to face such a paradox and to retain flexibility. They also wish to learn both old and new theories as well as share ideas about what might be the best approach to the unique situations with which they are constantly being faced. In this chapter, I will demonstrate how a peer group can be employed in the supervision of a multi-disciplinary group of therapeutic helpers. I will also give an example of how the group tackled a particular difficulty that faced one of its members.

The value of the peer group

The peer group has a most significant function in this respect and one can define the different ways in which such groups can come together and be of value. The main obvious advantage is in the enhancing of the efficiency of the work. It is now increasingly recognized, however, that such efficiency depends upon first, technical skills and second, less definable factors such as morale, a sense of identity and the quality of personal interactions between peers and between those higher or lower in the hierarchy of the particular institution concerned.

Two principal tasks of the peer group

It will be clear, therefore, that there are two closely interrelated tasks constantly taking place in the type of peer group referred to here which may be defined as: a group of people of similar status who are engaged in a similar line of work or in a cooperative project, who set aside regular committed time to examine the nature of the task and its effective accomplishment, and also examine those strengths and vulnerabilities – both as a group and as individuals – which may assist or inhibit the performance of the task.

The first aspect obviously requires a valuable sharing of skills and techniques and for some groups such as those in industry or commerce, the actual tasks will often be the main focus of attention. Even here, however, restrictive practices and unwillingness to share knowledge or teach skills to others can show a need to bring in the second aspect of the peer group.

This second aspect is more personal and recognizes that any job affects one's sense of identity. Kelly Howard (1984), in an article on the identity problems of those involved with alcohol, defined a 'lack of a sense of place' as being a major factor in human unhappiness. Those involved in counselling and all the helping professions will recognize the importance of this aspect of their own 'sense of place' in their work and how it is often difficult for those involved in such work to meet together and examine it. The confidential nature of the work tends to spark off personal reactions in a professional which are not always helpful to a client or colleagues. An essential element of this aspect is an understanding of psychodynamics and the way in which past, internalized, personal experience can be projected into the present and affect one's sense of acceptance as a valued team member.

The question of the absent leader

Yalom (1985) describes the value of what he similarly describes as the 'self directed' group and the proliferation of these in western society, especially in self-help organizations. He contrasts such a group with another type of leaderless group, used by some therapists as a deliberate strategy. In this type of group, the therapist withdraws regularly or intermittently to provide a leaderless session. The influence of the leader in such a group is still an active therapeutic force and this type of group is therefore not a peer group as being described here.

Yalom also lists the disadvantages of leaderless groups but points out that these are put forward by those familiar with working in groups with leaders. Most of the supposed disadvantages are related to the issue of dependency, which does not essentially need to be a main focus within the peer group, and is often, at least partially, resolved by the group's acceptance of the inevitable sense of vulnerability as difficult situations are approached.

In many of the groups facilitated by the author there has often been great surprise expressed that many of the problems such as projection, splitting and collusion do not appear with any great force. Such phenomena, when examined in a traditional psychotherapy group, can be the basis for the understanding of relationships as well as assisting in personal and professional development. In the peer group, however, it is more the psychodynamics of those involved in the actual situation being supervised which are the focus so that optimum change can occur as rapidly as possible. Personal therapy and more individual supervision may, of course, be valuable adjuncts to peer group supervision. The absence of a defined leader, authority figure or expert often provides a greater freedom to focus on the tasks external to the group and brought along for supervision whilst not ignoring the personal needs of group members so often thrown into sharp relief when working with those who are personally challenging to us.

Whatever the degree of a reassuring absence of imposed external power may be implied by the term 'peer', a fixed and finite equality is an impossibility and the term 'supervision' which is defined in the dictionary as 'watching over with authority' has, within its connotations, the idea that there may be a need for ground rules, principles, ethics and acquisition of skills which require the assent of all members. These may come from a sharing of the different and often hard-won experiences of others in the group or from new insights generated by the combined effort of the group members. There may also occasionally come from the group, as a whole, a desire to seek outside expertise from literature or from personalities well known for their experience. Members of such a peer group have often been sought for this type of consultation or training by other groups.

Peer group supervision, therefore, involves clear recognition of certain ground rules and authority. These will vary according to the personal needs of members for support, training and sharing of ideas. What is essential is to have agreement, from those in authority in the service, on guaranteed time being set aside with colleagues, without fear of ridicule or retribution. However, the danger lurking behind an exclusive concentration on personal needs is that the group becomes more and more divorced from the task – which in helping organizations is the welfare of the client. At worst, such a peer group becomes merely a focus for professional protectionism, an expression of a subversive sub-culture in which there is collusion to project all difficulties onto higher management or 'impossible' clients. It is here that concentration on the task being performed provides the discipline to look at the blocks in the performance of the task and how these can be ameliorated primarily by changes in the attitude and approach of the peer group members. After this has been done, it may then be easier to look at ways of negotiating changes in management and client situations but always from the perspective of task effectiveness. In this, the welfare and morale of staff may be of great importance but should rarely take precedence.

Forms of the peer group

In its simplest and most common form, a peer group meets for a morning coffee break, or in the pub after work, or more formally to plan a particular project. Such meetings are often more formalized than would at first appear and although it is easy for such groups simply to chat and bolster up each other's entrenched concepts, the author has nevertheless known of one group of workers where every Monday morning coffee break was designated as 'honesty time', when there was an undertaking that everyone would be given a chance to express any hidden or lingering discontent either about each other or about the working of the organization. This was not dissimilar from the ceremony of 'mea culpa' in convents when nuns, in turn, prostrate themselves in front of their sisters and admit to their sins and also listen to accusations concerning any sins which they may not have brought out. Whatever its advantages and disadvantages, this informal peer group is tending to become less common as coffee and lunch breaks become eroded and many people are very tired at the end of the day and prefer to unwind away from work and colleagues.

At the opposite extreme, but still perhaps classifiable as a 'peer group', is the situation where a group of workers meet but in the presence of an experienced or senior person. Even so, the aim is not primarily either management or a more classical type of analytic group with a leader taking the onus to train, support or interpret. Instead, concentration is upon facilitating the quality of the interaction and authentic communication of the group members which in turn can lead to the definition and achievement of the peer group's own personal or corporate goals. This can be a great advantage for cohesion and development of confidence at the commencement of the peer group.

A peer group for counselling and psychotherapy supervision

Between these two extremes it is possible to define a model for a peer group with commitment to a therapeutic search for meaning but which is relatively free, both of collusive friendship, and dependency on expert guidance –

although, as described below, this latter factor may be of value, especially in the early stages.

Such groups have been set up in Sheffield and other centres over the last 20 years and draw upon the experiences and ideas of writers such as Michael Balint and his colleagues who ran such groups for general practitioners (Balint *et al.* 1966) and medical students (Balint *et al.* 1969). Such an approach, in various modified forms, still influences many of those in the medical profession. The other important literature in this respect is that which studies institutions. This was initiated by Erving Goffman's (1961) classic work on the restrictions of fixed total institutions and Maxwell Jones's (1953) ideas showing how, by the use of therapeutic community principles, some of the worst of these restrictions can be overcome. Since then, there has been a plethora of written work on ways in which a more caring, and even more daring, exciting atmosphere can be engendered in what may, at first sight, seem a very mundane, established set-up. The author's own review (Gomersall 1988) focused on how feminine principles could be engendered with their combination of caring and creativity.

De Board (1978) showed how the various ideas of classical and more modern psychotherapies could be applied for the better functioning of business and industrial organizations. Today, charismatic authors such as Tom Peters (1987) put forward ideas which take into account the psychodynamic forces underlying human motivation. Such approaches can prove much more powerful than traditional 'carrot and stick' techniques based on engendering a climate consisting only of competition, obligation, blame and threat of punishment.

Practical aspects of the setting up of a peer group for supervision

The setting up of a peer group has some crucial elements which may recede in importance once it is established. Commitment of members to attend is the most important of these, and the author has found that in advising on the conduct of such groups, this is the most common reason for failure. Such a commitment does not simply consist of an intention on the part of members to be present: it means making attendance a first priority. Duties associated with work will always tend to have a force of precedence over attendance at the group and a member may feel that coming to the group is a personal indulgence. This is something which colleagues who are not members of the group may easily inflate since, as many workers in the field will know, envy of anything seen as 'personal help' is common. Deliberate attempts to sabotage peer groups have been made by such strategies as arranging other 'essential meetings' at the same time or even forbidding individuals to attend a peer group because it is not in some way 'recognized'.

Usually, sickness and annual holidays are accepted reasons for missing the group. Other reasons, such as appearing in Court, are quite understandable.

However, the commitment involves a trust within the group that all will attend and if issues associated with work get in the way, every support from other group members will be given to ensure that a member can overcome any obstacles to attendance. In some organizations, it is important to have a person in authority who will give their support to the group and explain its purpose and potential value to management who may be, understandably, wary of an hour of an employee's time being taken up in this way. It may be this same person who, as an actual member of the group, has a vital role in establishing a favourable climate for the group's work. Just as important as the commitment to attend is the commitment to bring greater awareness and meaning to bear on what happens in the group.

Growth of expertise in the peer group

In Balint's groups, the presence of a psychoanalyst was at first felt to be fundamental. However, many general practitioners, after several years of membership, found that they had developed and could, themselves, facilitate the sophisticated way of looking at individuals and situations which had been established by an analytic approach. This involved psychodynamic understanding of the influence of the past on those involved. It also involved looking at how past experience showed itself in issues of transference and countertransference. It was important to be able to take a systemic and holistic view of a situation and understand the interaction of the principal forces, looking at where these forces had their focus and how they could be changed. A facility for lateral thinking defined by De Bono (1982) was an important aspect of such a view.

The presence of a person such as an analyst need not be detrimental to the essential 'peer' element of the group. Their essential role is to share experience and knowledge and enhance the skill and knowledge already present in other group members. Care to avoid being seen as the focus of a parental, caring, directing or an interpretative role is necessary. If such a person brings their own clients or situations to the group for insightful discussion this can help avoid assumption of rigid roles, which can then become the shared responsibility of the group.

Size, admission and leaving arrangements

Another element of the set-up of the group is to have an agreed maximum size (ten is usual). Members take in turn the booking of a room and provision of tea and coffee. The same member reminds people of commitments and controls the start of serious discussion and insists on a strict finishing time. These are essential but not onerous administrative tasks. The eating of lunch during the group is quite detrimental except in rare individual cases of difficulty. An admission regime is required, usually consisting of a talk with two members who then report to the group their opinions and any possible sources of difficulty. A probationary system is also essential whereby a new member undertakes to attend for six consecutive sessions and observe the ground rules. At the end of this period, a request for continued membership may be made which will be agreed to if there are no evident problems.

Notice of intention to leave the group (of at least four weeks) is usually required. When the group reaches its maximum size and there are new members wishing to join, then two or three of the more experienced members may (reluctantly) face the challenge of setting up their own new peer group which, for a time, could run with those taking this initiative still being members of the original group. In such a way a system develops its own pattern of growth and its influence proliferates.

Ground rules

Ground rules of courtesy, confidentiality and listening until a person has clarified what they wish to say are necessary in addition to time, commitment and a willingness to look for meaning. Political correctness is not enforced but any expressions of prejudice, excessive idealization, projection and over-identification with any theory or movement are to be looked at for their psychodynamic aspects.

Interaction

The actual nature and substance of the interaction will obviously depend on the personalities of the members, their needs and the work with which they are involved. A certain discipline, coined from the model of the Balint group, to rapidly initiate a supervisory function on each occasion is necessary. In most groups experienced by the author, however, it has been important to allow ten minutes for members to make a cup of tea and abreact any current frustration in a socializing way before changing to the main function.

Rapidly, members develop the art of summarizing the objective elements of a case-history or situation. Case-notes are not brought into the group. From this emerges the actual core situation which the group member and/or the client is facing. This is facilitated by the group's questions, observations and speculations.

Sometimes, the nature of the supervisory process is a clarification of the dynamics of interaction in personal one-to-one therapy and the group member is enabled to see a developing pattern within the transference (often by reading their countertransference). This can lead to change and adjustment for the client. The links between this process and any other professional, statutory or medical involvement sometimes need careful scrutiny and assessment, trying to see where opportunities for therapeutic change exist rather than regretting the lack of an ideal situation.

In groups with a mixture of members of core professions who may not be practising exclusively as individual therapists, the combination of roles is further complicated by the interactions of many 'dramatis personae' who are clustered around the client in question. It is here that a chalk board or large piece of paper become especially valuable in charting out the individuals and forces concerned. Psychodrama, sculpting, art therapy and sand tray pictures may all be used to similar effect. A mandala type of representation, showing forces which work towards harmony and understanding (depicted as acting centripetally towards the centre) and forces causing separation and disharmony (depicted as acting centrifugally towards the periphery) may be useful.

Clinical example of peer group help using a mandala

A mandala representation will be made clear by referring to two diagrams which give an example of a quite common scenario in many 'helping' situations. This method of representation and charting can easily be adapted to other presenting scenarios.

In this example, a group member, John, a community mental health nurse, had been asked by the consultant in his team to assess and work with a family whose adolescent daughter, Jane, aged 18, had taken an overdose. He had made his first visit two days before bringing the case to the group. John was experienced in formal family therapy and had managed to get most of the family together including mother and father, who were middle-aged and employed in the local cutlery industry, as well as Jane's younger brother, aged 14, who was still at school. The family dog, Mitchum, was present, but grandmother, who lived across the road, declined to come. It emerged that Jane felt that she had always been treated as inferior because she was a girl and her younger brother had been favoured. Since leaving school six months previously, she had not managed to get a job, had few friends and spent most of the day watching television. She used to visit grandmother but recently they had quarrelled. She had given the reason for the overdose to the consultant on his brief home visit as feeling 'useless and unwanted'. This is just what Kelly Howard (1984) describes as having a 'lost sense of place'.

The individual and family psychodynamics emerged clearly in subsequent visits and in the supervision sessions. What was valuable at this first description, however, was the capacity of John, with the help of the group, to share his initial uncomfortable, lonely role. Jane had remained angry and miserable with outbursts of temper alternating with sullen withdrawal and continued threats of suicide. The family were furious because they had expected the consultant to admit Jane and he had not even 'given her an antidepressant'. Her younger brother referred to her as a 'nutter' but the dog, Mitchum, stayed beside Jane most of the time.

Figure 10.1 shows a composite effort of the group produced at the initial supervisory session. The various attitudes, roles and anxieties of those involved are shown. This was then, however, placed beside a modification in Figure 10.2, of Karpman's 'victim, rescuer, persecutor triangle' (1968), and showed how powerfully operative were the presenting roles (represented by the thick double lines) sometimes emerging as fixed pathological roles, shown peripherally, which prevented any change of harmony or healing exchanges within the family. This was particularly evident in the countertransference

Opting out

Consultant
Dosen't care. Unwilling to use his power

John
who is seen as having 'inferior power'

No collusion here by **John** which would have disempowered the family

Negating all 'help'

Jane
victim

Father
Jane's brother
Persecutors

Denigrating

Mother
combining both attempts at 'rescuer' and 'victim' in the use of 'martyr' strategies. At first saw John as a 'rival rescuer'

John
avoids heavy-handed 'prescriptive' helping

John
Rescuer. Avoided helping in absence of understanding what was going on. **Mitchum** was a non-pathological 'rescuer'

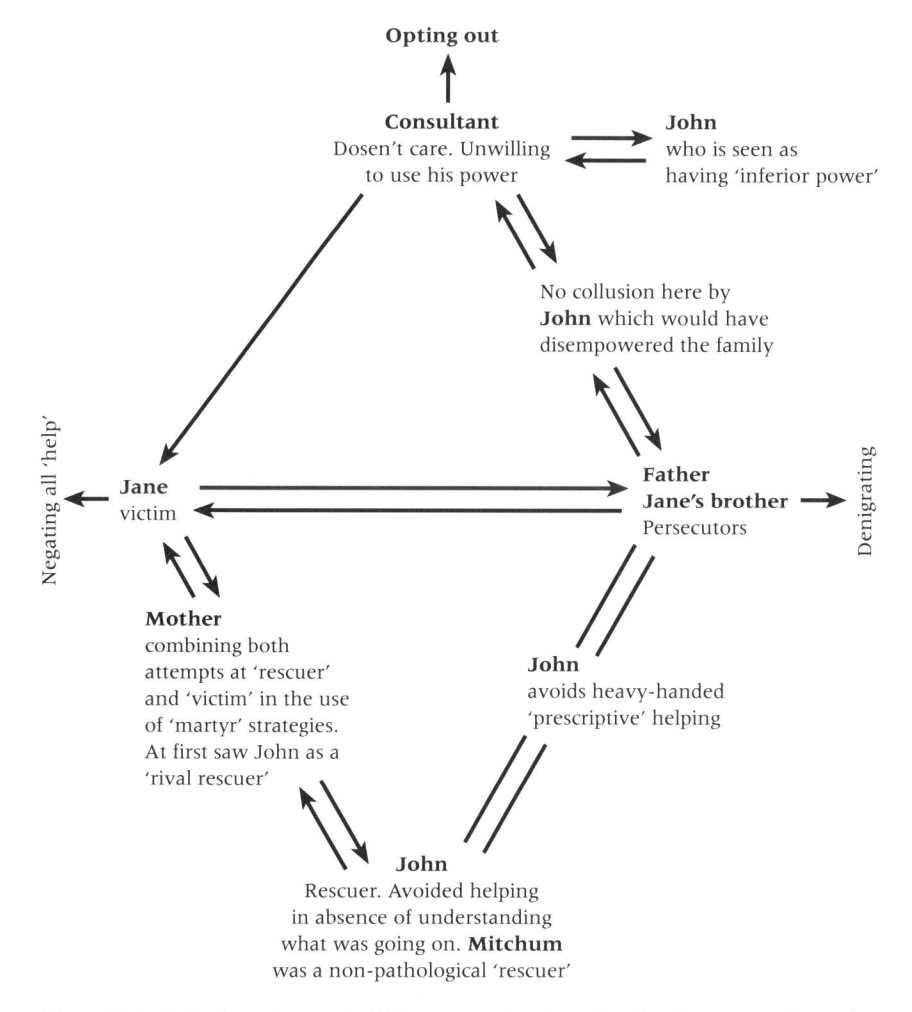

Figure 10.1 This shows how at initial presentation those involved were seen by each to occupy pathologically reinforcing roles. The therapist, John, was in danger of being drawn into this, mainly at the points shown, but refused to become enmeshed.

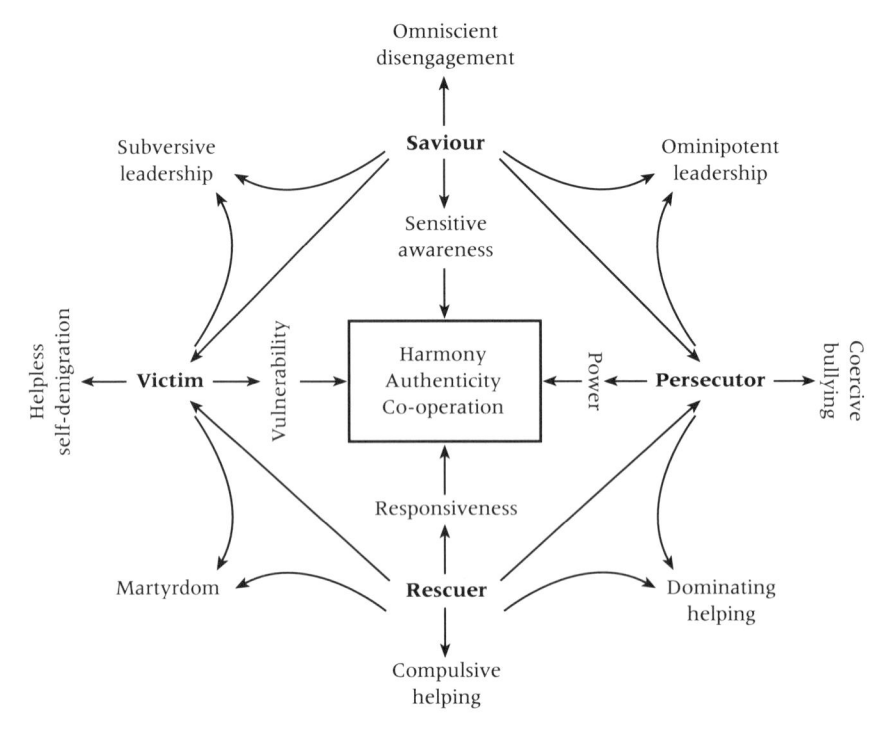

```
                        Omniscient
                        disengagement
                             ↑
         Subversive       Saviour        Omnipotent
         leadership   ↖           ↗      leadership
                          Sensitive
                          awareness
                             ↓
                       ┌──────────┐
            Helpless   │ Harmony  │         Coercive
   ← Victim →  Vulnerability │ Authenticity │ ← Power ← Persecutor →  bullying
    self-denigration   │ Co-operation │
                       └──────────┘
                             ↑
                       Responsiveness
         Martyrdom  ↙            ↘   Dominating
                        Rescuer          helping
                             ↓
                        Compulsive
                         helping
```

Figure 10.2 This is a modification of Stephen Karpman's original concept of the 'victim, rescuer, persecutor triangle'. By superimposing Figure 10.1 upon this, it is possible to see how the family concerned played out their roles.

Karpman's later idea that each negative role has hidden and unusual healing potential opens the way for insightful therapeutic working.

The author's 'mandala' representation shows the forces of harmony pointing towards the centre, and forces of disharmony and separative conflict pointing towards the periphery where they can become fixed in the types of well-known strategies labelled here.

feelings of John, who went into the family as potential rescuer and saviour but rapidly found himself seen as persecutor (one who couldn't or wouldn't give the expected solution), and then as victim, of all family members except Mitchum, who greeted John with excessive friendliness.

The modification of Karpman's triangle shown at the top with the addition of 'saviour' and the roles of 'subversive' and 'omnipotent' leaders rapidly disappeared, in the case of this family. It was a help that the consultant had been of no use, and that the father's simple formula about how good daughters 'should' behave was rejected by all the rest. The family had reluctantly agreed to a second full one-hour session with John. This time each started talking and listening to descriptions of their roles and sometimes even expressing their fears. They began to see how these roles had been reinforcing each other within the lower part of the figure – Karpman's original triangle. Thus this original triangle was sufficient for adequate understanding. The main therapeutic element here which John was able to bring along, in addition to his interest and commitment to spend time helping the family to look for meaning, was a supportive respect for each person and what each of them was saying. Strangely, Mitchum was a valuable role symbol for this and was already respected and could give respect all round, particularly to the most victimized person.

The concept of each pathological role in Karpman's model having a hidden therapeutic aspect, which is usually denied, is a valuable one. In the case of this family, once recognized, it brought about a rapid resolution of the tense, mutually denigrating situation which had grown up. Thus, mother recognized that her main role of martyr, which combined her role of hard-pressed, coping family manager (rescuer) with victim, was seen by the others as persecutory. It also denied the other female member any sense of place and value. Mother admitted her hidden sense of vulnerability and her ready responsiveness to situations which she began to both value and share with Jane as she spoke openly about her constantly threatened family of origin.

All the family became more attuned to what others wanted and co-operated with their new found 'response-ability'. Traditionally, father had been the main persecutor, overtly expressing anger and denigration of all the others. He was accepted as having power in that he earned money and did many practical things in the home. This power began to be shared. All began to take a serious overall look at family finances and the need for everyone to have a fair share for themselves and yet to make reasonable contributions to family welfare, financial and otherwise. Jane's brother was seen to have colluded with father in the persecution of Jane and with mother in allowing the latter to remove Jane's responsibilities. He admitted his vulnerability, which came over as a fear of becoming the victim, if Jane once lost this role.

Jane, having heard the rest of the family relinquish their tightly cast roles, was enabled to take a part in family decisions. She no longer sabotaged these by negativism, tantrums and refusal to join in any of the family's ventures. An important symbolic event in achieving this was, simply, everyone taking a walk with Mitchum. The dog was no longer the only one who shared Jane's misery, and dashed from one to the other as if in celebration of Jane no longer needing his exclusive affection.

The peer group's attempt to understand organizations

Where one is dealing with pathological communications within organizations in whose machinations individuals tend to become caught up, then the quadrilateral representation rather than the triangle, with one person taking on, or being forced into, the role of saviour, can become relevant. Sometimes such a person acts with unquestioned but skilled authority but, unfortunately, as shown at the very top of Figure 10.2, such a saviour leader is distant and unavailable. Also, as indicated on the top right aspect of the figure, an element of bullying and coercion can creep in. The other powerful aspect of this saviour role is when it is taken over by one or more people in a sub-culture, as shown at the top left aspect of the figure. A common example of this is where new members of an organization are taken aside by 'fixers' and old hands and taught ways to subvert and 'use' the working of the organization to the benefit of its more junior staff. Awkward blocked relationships often develop with middle management, to the detriment of the institution. Tom Peters (1987) points out how important it is for such blocks to be broken apart by middle management.

Conclusion

Peer group supervision as described here is not a substitute for personal therapy and intensive regular individual supervision. It can, however, be a relatively low-cost endeavour which is easy to organize. It generates great enthusiasm once members of a group become committed to each other and to the holistic, eclectic understanding of situations in which they come to see themselves playing powerful key therapeutic roles. It is particularly valuable in those organizations where a climate of psychodynamic understanding is only just beginning to emerge from one dominated by a climate of blame and mistrust, rewards and punishments: where heavy organization from above and a lack of mutual support predominate. Similarly, it can help in situations in which support comes only from a subversive subculture which is purely staff protective.

References

Balint, M., Ball, D.H. and Hare, M.L. (1969) Training medical students in patient-centred medicine. *Comprehensive Psychiatry*, 10: 249.
Balint, M., Balint, E., Gosling, R. and Hildebrand, P. (1966) *A Study of Doctors*. London: Tavistock Publications.
De Board, R. (1978) *The Psychoanalysis of Organizations*. London: Tavistock Publications.
De Bono, E. (1982) *De Bono's Thinking Course*. London: British Broadcasting Corporation.
Goffman, E. (1961) *Asylums*. New York: Doubleday Anchor.
Gomersall, J. (1988) Introducing a feminine balance within our institutions, in D. Glasgow and N. Eisenberg (eds) *Current Issues in Clinical Psychology*. London: Gower.
Howard, K. (1984) Hey Ma. Someone's standing in my swamp. *Counselling*, 48: 15–20.
Jones, M. (1953) *The Therapeutic Community*. New York: Basic Books.
Karpman, S.B. (1968) Fairy tales and script drama analysis. *Transactional Analysis Journal*, 1: 39–43.
Peters, T. (1987) *Thriving on Chaos*. New York: Knopf Inc.
Szasz, T. (1965) *The Ethics of Psychoanalysis*. London: Routledge & Kegan Paul.
Yalom, I.D. (1985) *The Theory and Practice of Group Psychotherapy*. New York: Basic Books.

11

THETRIANGLE WITH CURVED SIDES: SENSITIVITY TO ISSUES OF RACE AND CULTURE IN SUPERVISION

Colin Lago and Joyce Thompson

> At present those who teach methods of supervision or supervise work with non-traditional clients rely on underdeveloped literature, unvalidated personal experiences and knowledge, and trial and error practice guided hopefully by keenly attuned empathy and clinical wisdom in addressing issues of race and culture within counselling supervision.
> (Thompson 1991, p. 6)

Introduction

Individual counsellors and psychotherapists have long expressed their concerns as to their competency and sensitivity when working with racially and culturally different clients. These individual concerns became successfully articulated and recognized at organizational levels through several key conferences and committee structures during the late 1970s in the United Kingdom. Examples of these within the British Association for Counselling (BAC) include the chosen theme of the national conference in 1979, addressing the therapeutic needs of minority groups. Initially, in preparation for that conference, and subsequently, as a structured attempt to further understanding, a multi-disciplinary, multi-racial group of mental health professionals, based in Leicester, met to exchange ideas, generate training concerns and media and, in the process, enhance their own knowledge of and sensitivity to the complexities of trans-cultural counselling.

At about the same time, concerns were also raised at the annual conference of the Counselling in Education Division of BAC by the one black delegate present. The emerging cumulative concerns eventually found expression in formal policy statements of commitment by the British Association for Counselling and the subsequent formation of a formal sub-committee of BAC, entitled 'Race Awareness in Counselling Education' (RACE), to oversee developments in this field. During the early 1980s the Association of Black

Counsellors (ABC) was also formed and this provided an appropriate forum for serious discussion of the issues of race and culture and the specific implications these may have for black therapists. Since then a variety of articles, chapters and books on this subject have been published within Britain (D'Ardenne and Mahtani 1989; Lago and Thompson 1989; Eleftheriadou 1994). Joyce Thompson, through a Master's degree research project, chose to pursue her understanding of these particular issues as they impacted upon the supervisory relationship. Some of these considerations inform the early part of this chapter.

The impact of race and culture upon therapy

Concerns about sensitive and informed trans-cultural therapeutic practice have now been expressed over several decades within the United States, both through publications and through organizational policy. Key American theorists include Sue (1981), Atkinson (1985), Pedersen (1987a), and Lee and Richardson (1991). The issues that are raised when a client from one cultural/racial background meets a therapist of a different cultural and racial origin are multifarious, complex and indeed challenging to the very belief that counselling can be helpful in such circumstances. A matrix for the explorations of these dynamics is shown in Figure 11.1 (see also Lago and Thompson 1989).

Through the exploration of the likely phenomena that might occur between each of these four therapeutic pairings, a wide range of data was revealed that could negatively impact upon the therapeutic process. Such issues included: ignorance, projections, negative attribution, power relations, racism, stereotyping, language usage, sense of racial identity, the relevance of the impact of culturally determined theoretical position and so on. This latter point has been considered by Pedersen (1987a) and more recently by Lago and Thompson (1996).

The matrix deliberately over-simplifies the cross-racial dyad as a means of articulating the issues. Once one adds the phenomena of cultural difference

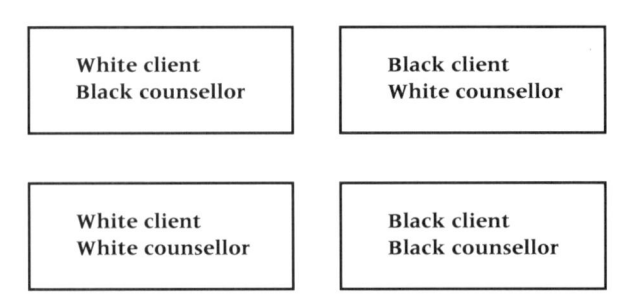

White client Black counsellor	Black client White counsellor
White client White counsellor	Black client Black counsellor

Figure 11.1 The supervisory matrix

and identity to the therapeutic relationship the sheer complexity of the therapeutic endeavour is magnified dramatically. Such examples include systems of thought and belief, use of language, paralinguistic and non-verbal behaviour, cultural assumptions, use of kinship support systems in therapy, philosophies of life, patterns of child rearing, roles of men and women, attitudes about time, polite behaviour, what constitutes a problem, methods of help-seeking, etc.

An expanding range of literature is now available upon this extremely complex and challenging aspect of counselling and psychotherapy. Based upon such a brief exposition of the therapeutic relationship one may see, perhaps, with appropriate alarm and apprehension, a formidable expansion in the degrees and levels of complexity and potential misunderstanding when the supervisory role is considered in relation to the trans-cultural/trans-racial counselling relationship.

The complexity of trans-cultural/trans-racial supervision

> Ideally, supervisors should have a reservoir of positive and non-positive therapeutic experiences with non-traditional clients from which to draw instructive, anxiety reducing and insight inducing, examples. It is critical that supervisors have special knowledge of and empathy for the client whose therapy s/he is to supervise regardless of race and culture in order to enhance good practice.
>
> (Thompson 1991, p. 6)

Batten (1990) has already noted that the impact of migration patterns and cultural diversity within contemporary society will drive the need to understand more fully what the implications are for supervision when the therapist and supervisor are of different cultural and racial origins. Holloway (1989) has explored the power relationship in supervision and notes its special relevance within this context where the supervisor is white and the therapist black. By virtue of their whiteness and through being a member of the dominant majority, the supervisor carries or represents personal and societal power. In addition, the role of supervisor carries professional power. This graphic imbalance of power position is demonstrated in research by Vandervolk (1974) in the United States reporting that, prior to any supervision, black supervisees anticipated less supervisor empathy, respect and congruence than white supervisees. The evidence supported the possibility that a supervisee's race and culture may be a source of potential conflict in the supervisory relationship.

Helms (1982) also found that a predominantly white sample of supervisors perceived that supervisees who were 'people of color' (a term used in the United States to refer to non-whites), were less able to accept constructive criticism, less open to self-examination and as having more problems in keeping appointments than white supervisees. However, in contrast to white supervisees, supervisees of colour evaluated themselves more positively on these dimensions than did their supervisors.

These findings indicate that trans-cultural/trans-racial supervisory dyads will tend to be more conflictual than racially/culturally homogeneous pairings and that supervisors may also contribute to that conflict. Such differences of perspective will not only affect the supervisor/supervisee relationship but could negatively affect the supervisee's therapeutic relationship with their client. Given that the majority of supervisors in Britain are white, black therapists may experience considerable dissatisfaction with their supervisory relationship.

Atkinson *et al.* (1983) suggested that supervisors needed to have some general knowledge about:

- the process of formation of racial and cultural identities[1]
- cultural norms
- the nature of conflicts between blacks and whites;
- and a willingness to address how their supervisees manage anxiety in situations where cultural and racial differences are present.

Hunt (1986) suggests that a culturally sensitive supervisor understands these differences and can help supervisees learn facilitative behaviour in trans-cultural interactions.

The triangular relationship

As an aid to exploring the implications of race and culture for the supervisory process, Joyce Thompson (1991) developed a series of triangular diagrams depicting the various supervisor/counsellor/client relationships where racial/cultural difference is an element (see Figure 11.2).

The broken lines shown between supervisor and client represent the supervisors' 'overseeing' function, to see that the client is not being harmed by the therapeutic process and that there is no direct communication between the two of them (i.e. supervisor and client). Taking one diagram at a time, a training group would be able to brainstorm a wide range of issues that are likely to impede the communication processes between the three different participants – the client, the therapist and the supervisor, especially in circumstances of racial and cultural difference.

The curved side

We have chosen this term to help us describe what can happen to the communication process between people generally, but more specifically between cross-racial or cross-cultural pairings. This perspective is supported by Winnicott's ideas of false self identification (1965) and Rogers' theory of personality development (1959).[2]

THE TRIANGLE WITH CURVED SIDES 123

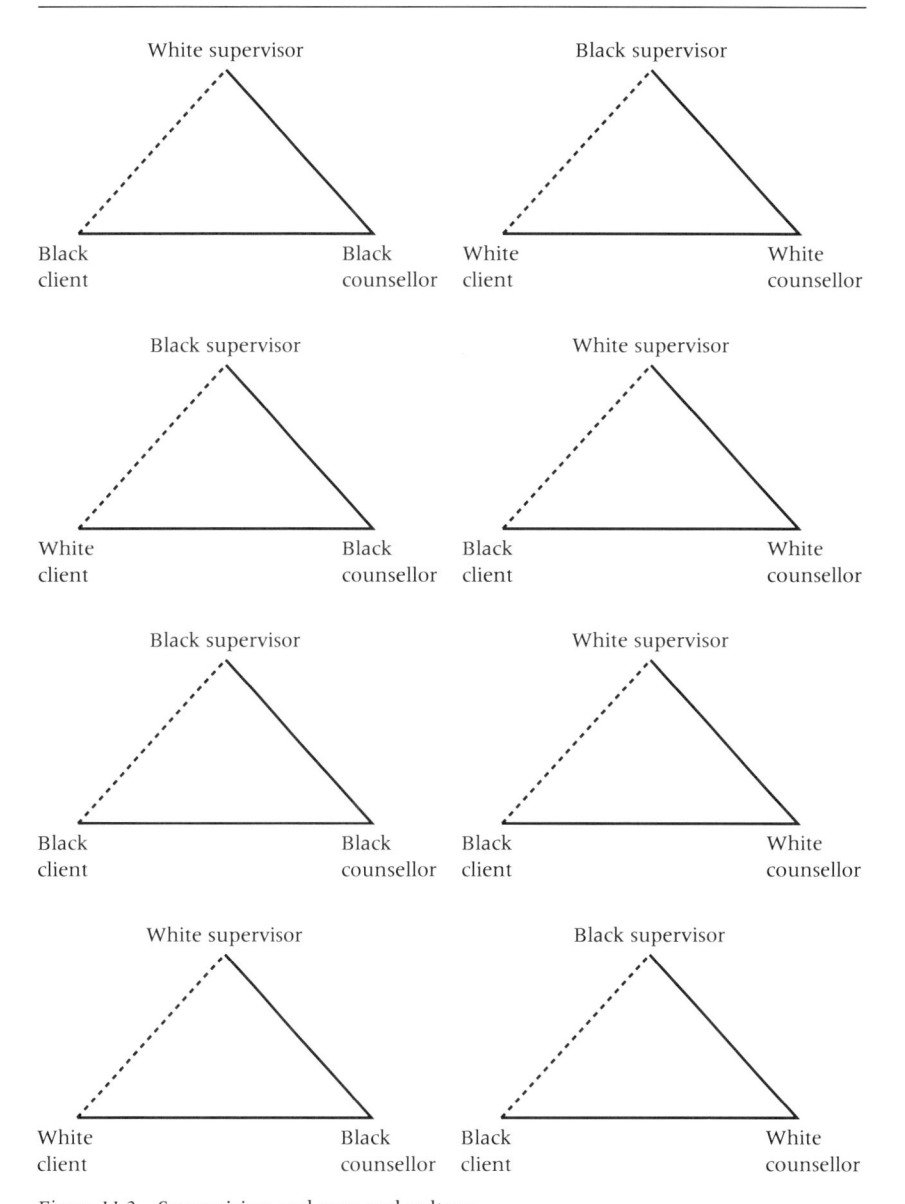

White supervisor	Black supervisor
Black client — Black counsellor	White client — White counsellor
Black supervisor	White supervisor
White client — Black counsellor	Black client — White counsellor
Black supervisor	White supervisor
Black client — Black counsellor	Black client — White counsellor
White supervisor	Black supervisor
White client — Black counsellor	Black client — White counsellor

Figure 11.2 Supervision and race and culture

Let us consider one example, that of a white therapist with a black client. The white therapist is a symbolic representative of white society and therefore, at some level, represents all that this might mean including discrimination and racism. The black client, being a member of a visible minority

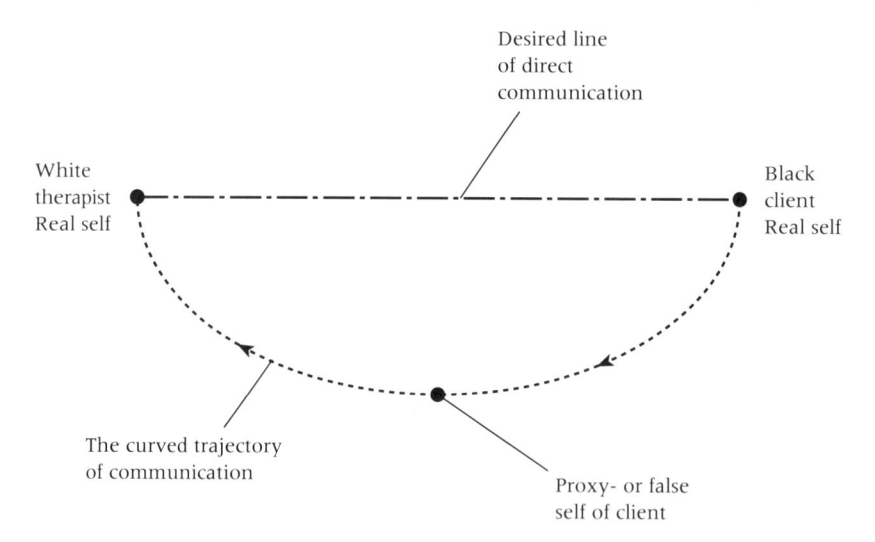

Figure 11.3 Client–therapist communication

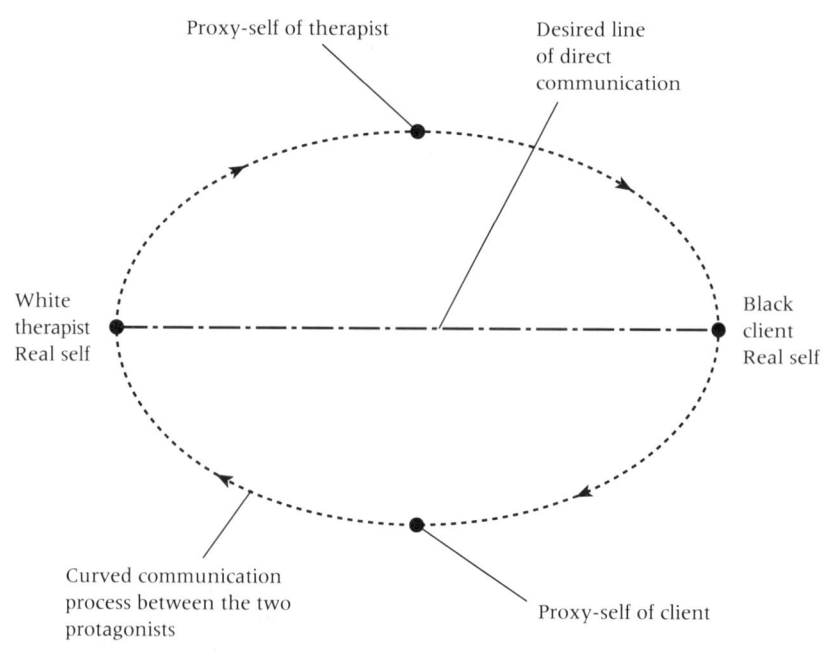

Figure 11.4 Proxy-self and real self communication

group, has had to learn to project a 'front', a proxy-self, that ensures their survival in, and acceptability to, white society, in order to protect their real self. We are thus using the term 'proxy-self' here to mean that aspect of self that is presented most often to the outside world. This 'self' presentation will

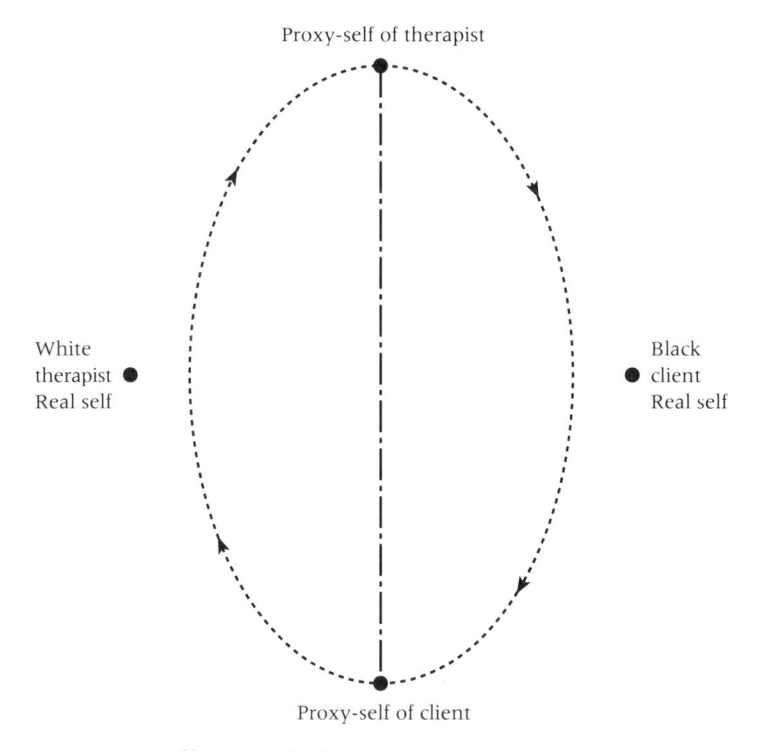

Figure 11.5 Proxy-self communication

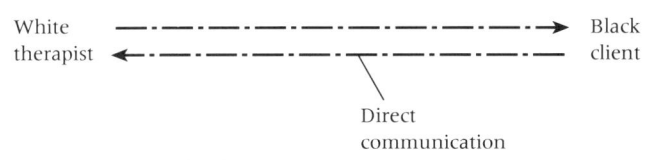

Figure 11.6 Direct communication

comprise behaviours that are both consciously and unconsciously determined, based on the client's past experiences. In the above example, the black client's previous experiences of white people will affect how they present themself to a white therapist. Diagrammatically, the resulting communication process from client to therapist can be depicted in Figure 11.3.

Figure 11.3, however, is too biased or one-sided as a diagram. Many white therapists working in a trans-racial/trans-cultural relationship will be anxious to demonstrate that they can be helpful to the client; that they are not like other whites (who may be oppressive, prejudiced, etc.); that they do accept the client; that they do understand, and so on. Needing to project these positive aspects of their personality, however sincerely intended, will nevertheless also entrap them in a projection of their proxy-self. Consequently the full diagram of communication looks like Figure 11.4.

The curved communication process between the two participants is in many ways less desirable but seems almost inevitable in the early stages of the development of this therapeutic relationship. Indeed, the worst outcome of this configuration will be a communication pattern and relationship that only functions via the proxy-selves, as depicted in Figure 11.5, and then gets stuck within this framework.

As time and trust develop in this relationship, the curved communication process through the client's and the therapist's proxy-selves may be reduced to more direct communication between the two, as shown in Figure 11.6.

The triangular relationship with curved sides

For the purposes of simple representation, an example of the communication pattern between therapist and client was taken. If we apply these patterns to the triangular relationship of supervisor, therapist and client, an increasingly complex pattern emerges! These are represented in Figures 11.7–11.9.

A further detail of complexity in these communication patterns is the possibility that the supervisor also develops a false view of the client and the client's difficulties. This view will be generated, in part only, by their receipt of information from the therapist's proxy-self. The additional, false perspectives (if the supervisor is untrained and unaware) will come from their own lack of knowledge of the client's cultural norms, relevant ideas about racial identity development, and their own defences against the therapist's anxieties and feared impotence in dealing with culturally and racially different clients. This is represented in Figure 11.10.

The diagrams will hopefully not prove to be too complicated to comprehend. They are meant to depict the idea that in communicating with someone else, we put on a 'presentable face' (proxy-self) which we think is acceptable to them. In trans-racial and trans-cultural situations, especially where the participants hail from a dominant and a minority group within society, a configuration of relations through proxy-selves is very likely to occur. Given the sheer volume of research data that supports a view of western society as one that is discriminatory and racist, this implies that minority persons have to work out ways of surviving physically and psychologically. It is therefore not at all surprising that cross-cultural communication in therapy is so complex. These ideas are also understandable from the perspectives of both analytic and client-centred theories of personality.

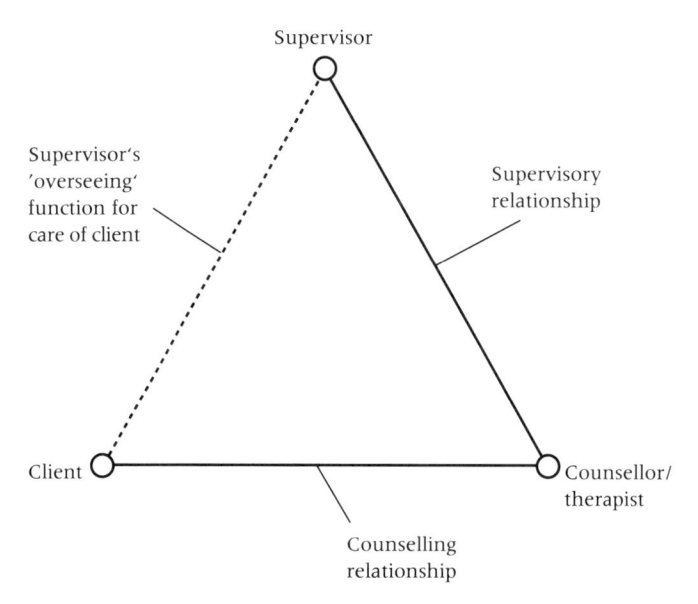

Figure 11.7 The most direct relationship

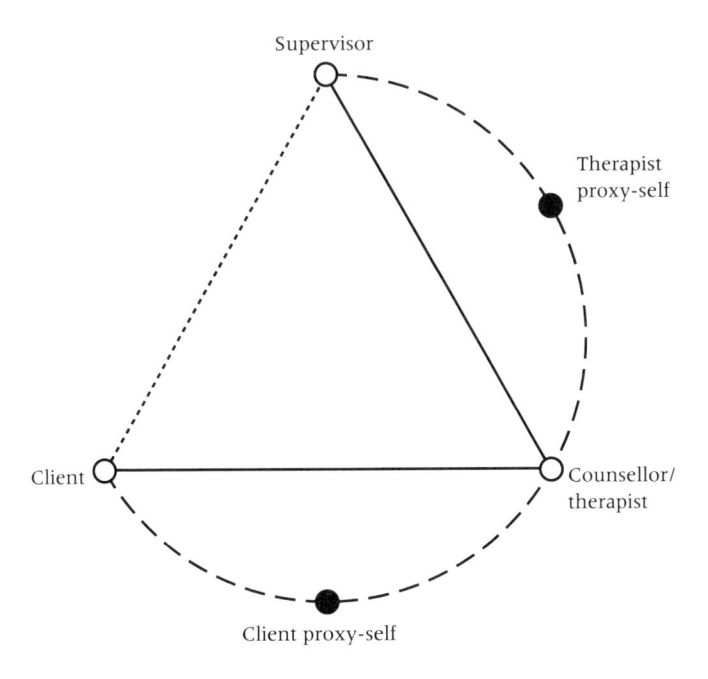

Figure 11.8 The addition of the proxy-self idea to the supervisory relationship

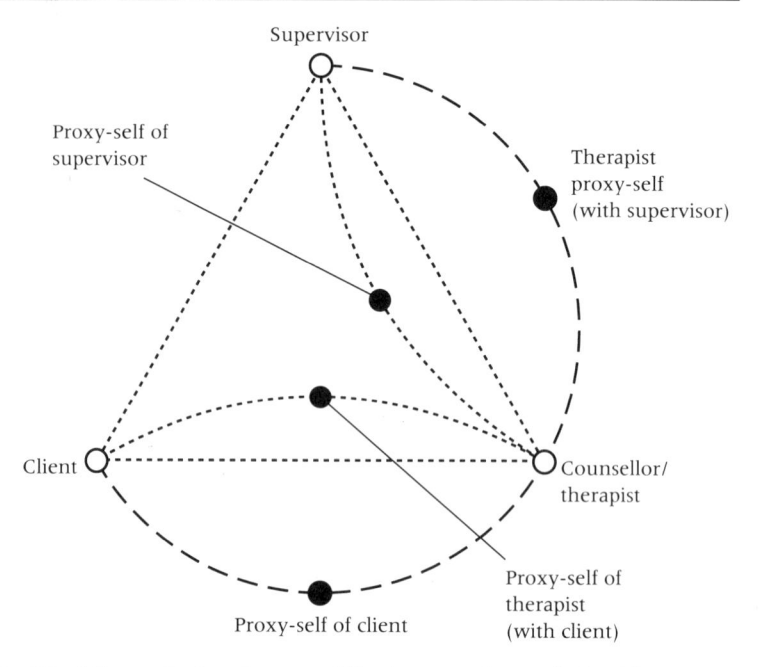

Figure 11.9 The full complexity of proxy-self in the supervisory relationship

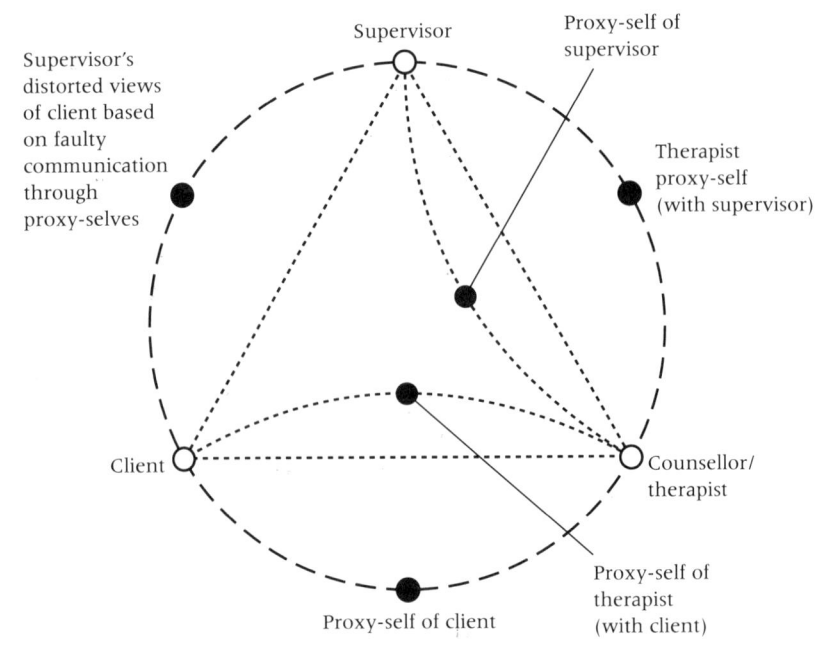

Figure 11.10 The triangle with curved sides

Summing up

This chapter began by referring to the complexities of trans-cultural/trans-racial therapy. Despite its clinical advisability and ethical necessity, we have also demonstrated that the superimposition of the supervisory relationship upon a trans-racial/trans-cultural therapy relationship cannot be assumed to be a smooth one. At worst, all three parties may never get close to the core issues that originally impelled the client to enter therapy. We have demonstrated also that this incapacity to relate and communicate deeply may occur even when the state of intention from all three perspectives is honourable and professional. Malign intent, even if from unconscious sources, does not have to exist for there to be negative or unhelpful outcomes. Trans-cultural/trans-racial supervision poses many questions and much more research work is urgently required to illuminate these potentially complex processes.

Notes

1 All the work on these models of identity development has been carried out within the United States and the models are presented well in Ponterotto and Pedersen (1993). They have been described as being at the 'leading edge' of trans-cultural therapeutic practice (Lee 1994). Individuals from oppressed minorities may assume and experiment with 'trial identities' before coming to their own sense of integration as visible black members of a predominantly white culture.
2 We are most grateful to Dr Lennox Thomas who stimulated these ideas in a lecture to the RACE Division of the British Association for Counselling in 1994.

References

Atkinson, D. (1985) A meta-review of research on cross-cultural counselling and psychotherapy. *Journal of Multicultural Counseling & Development*, 13: 138–53.

Atkinson, D., Morton, G. and Sue, D.W. (1983) *Counseling American Minorities: A cross cultural perspective*. Dubuque, IA: Williams C. Brown.

Batten, C. (1990) Dilemmas of crosscultural psychotherapy supervision. *British Journal of Psychotherapy*, 7(2): 129–40.

D'Ardenne, P. and Mahtani, A. (1989) *Transcultural Counselling in Action*. London: Sage.

Eleftheriadou, Z. (1994) *Transcultural Counselling*. London: Central Book Publishing.

Helms, J. (1982) 'Differential evaluations of minority and majority counseling trainees practicum performance', unpublished manuscript. University of Maryland.

Holloway, E. (1989) 'Engagement and Power in Clinical Supervision', unpublished thesis. University of Oregon.

Hunt, P. (1986) Black clients. Implications for supervision of trainees. *Psychotherapy*, 24: 161–4.

Lago, C.O. and Thompson, J. (1989) Counselling and race, in W. Dryden, D. Charles-Edwards and R. Wolfe (eds) *Handbook of Counselling in Britain*. London: Tavistock/Routledge.

Lago, C.O. and Thompson. J. (1996) *Race, Culture and Counselling*. Buckingham: Open University Press.

Lee, C.C. (1994) 'Recent research in transcultural counselling', paper presented at 'Race, Culture and Counselling' conference, University of Sheffield.

Lee, C.C. and Richardson, B.L. (eds) (1991) *Multicultural Issues in Counseling: New approaches to diversity.* Alexandria, VA: American Association for Counseling and Development.

Pedersen, P.B. (1987a) *Handbook of Cross-Cultural Counseling and Therapy*. New York: Praeger.

Pedersen, P.B. (1987b) Ten frequent assumptions of cultural bias in counseling. *Journal of Multicultural Counseling and Development*, January: 16–24.

Ponterotto, J.G. and Pedersen, P.B. (1993) *Preventing Prejudice: A guide for counselors and educators*. Newbury Park: Sage.

Rogers, C.R. (1959) A theory of therapy, personality, and interpersonal relationships, as developed in the client-centered framework, in S. Koch (ed.) *Psychology: A study of a science, formulations of the person and the social context*. New York: McGraw Hill.

Sue, D.W. (1981) *Counseling the Culturally Different: Theory and practice*. New York: John Wiley and Sons, Inc.

Thompson, J. (1991) 'Issues of race and culture in counselling supervision training courses', unpublished MSc dissertation, Polytechnic of East London.

Vandervolk, C. (1974) The relationship of personality, values and race to anticipation of the supervisory relationship. *Rehabilitation Counselling Bulletin*, 18: 41–6.

Winnicott, D.W. (1965) *The Maturational Processes and the Facilitating Environment*. London: Hogarth.

12

BECOMING A SUPERVISOR

Deborah Pickvance

This chapter looks at the process involved in becoming a supervisor. It pays special attention to the issues which a therapist who is beginning to undertake supervision may consider in preparation for the role. The dynamics of the supervisory relationship are discussed, with reference to their possible effects on a relationship between a new supervisor and a supervisee.

A supervisor is a significant figure in the training of a therapist and usually in the therapist's ongoing working life. A supervisor can have a particularly strong influence in the development of a trainee therapist, and supervision still plays an important function in the work of experienced therapists. Yet there is little preparation specifically for the role and many supervisors have minimal or no training for it. The transition from therapist to supervisor usually goes unheralded and unmarked; there are no rites of passage as the therapist takes on the new role. Until recently, as Mander (1993: 1) has written, 'supervision was not recognized as a distinct professional activity that would deserve specific examination as to its processes, methods and products'. Little has been written about the change from therapist to supervisor and, as Mander (1993: 1) points out, 'the assumption was that any experienced therapist could give supervision, as if this was merely an extension of the therapeutic metier'. This has meant that supervisors have had 'to capitalize on various and incidental learning processes as the major modality by which supervision is learnt' (Hess 1986: 58). However, there is increasing recognition that the role of supervisor differs from the role of therapist in significant ways, which are described below, and therefore that specific training in supervision can help a therapist who wants to become a supervisor. The growing number of training courses in supervision reflects that awareness.

Reasons for becoming a supervisor

Therapists decide to become supervisors for a variety of reasons, some obvious and some less tangible. Often it is a requirement of a job to supervise trainee therapists or therapists with less experience. A therapist may become a supervisor not through a planned career move but simply in response to a request by another therapist for supervision.

Ideally, therapists have to have confidence in their own abilities, as well as a desire to participate in the professional development of another therapist and a willingness to take on the challenge of supervising. Undertaking supervision is a way for therapists to diversify their work, to continue to engage with the therapeutic process but at one step removed. Alonso (1983: 28) described a sense of relief expressed by supervisors at being able in supervision 'to work in the conscious, cognitive, progressive levels of communications . . . as opposed to the work with patients that is complicated and made more difficult by the need to uncover the murky layers of the unconscious'.

Therapists may be motivated by a sense of having something to offer, of feeling ready to begin to supervise. It can be difficult to gauge this feeling as there is no benchmark against which to measure it. A therapist may also be driven by more narcissistic needs and become a supervisor out of a desire for the status and prestige that the role confers or because of the flattery and gratification of being asked. Therapists may wish to prove their competence or pursue their personal ambition. A further motivation may lie in the opportunity provided by supervision 'to assuage our object hunger – this is such an occupational hazard among psychodynamic clinicians – a chance to meet nice people, to not be so lonely' (Alonso 1983: 28). Therapists may undertake supervision out of a wish to reap the satisfactions and pleasures which the job offers. As Alonso describes:

> And ultimately, we supervise because it's fun! It's exciting to make order out of chaos, to watch the contagious excitement of our students, and to share in the intimate pleasure of contact over emotional growth and expansion; it's fun to watch someone move from student to colleague, and watch the better parts of ourselves move into posterity.
>
> (1983: 28)

The role of supervisor and preparation for it

One way in which supervision differs from therapy is that the supervisor has to imagine the client and then work with the imagined client. The supervisor tries to understand a client from listening to the supervisee, to assess the nature of the client's difficulties and their possible effects on the client's relationship with the therapist. In addition to managing the supervisory relationship, the supervisor also evaluates the supervisee's competence, strengths and weaknesses and consequent needs from supervision. The supervisor develops a flexible approach, offering a balance of support and challenge which enables the supervisee to explore anxieties and defences and also to recognize and develop their strengths. Langs (1980: 109) writes that: 'The supervisor should be capable of gentle but candid work which sensitively acquaints the supervisee not only with the nature of his main difficulties as a therapist, but with his unrecognized assets as well.'

Therapists can prepare themselves for the new role by evaluating what they bring to it and identifying the areas which they feel they need to develop. Styczynski (1980) describes the resources which a therapist brings to the supervisory role; for example, previous learning as a supervisee which gives the therapist experience of a variety of role models and also understanding of how some aspects of supervision are more useful than others. Experience in teaching gives the supervisor skill in the evaluation of the learning needs of students as well as familiarity with the roles of authority and mentor. Skill as a therapist is a crucial resource which helps the supervisor in guiding the supervisee to make successful therapeutic interventions and also in structuring the supervisory relationship. Research experience can be useful in developing skills in accurate observation and in integrating observation into formulations of clients' problems. As a colleague and consultant, the new supervisor already has experience of trying to understand clients on the basis of listening to another person's account and, also, of giving and receiving feedback in a mutually respectful way.

It takes time for a beginning supervisor to become accustomed to the new professional role. The impact of becoming a supervisor varies with the level of experience of the therapist. Experienced therapists find it less stressful than recently qualified ones, who, despite their relative lack of experience, may be expected to supervise within their job (Hess 1986). However, in a review of changes in supervision as supervisors gain experience, Worthington (1987) found little evidence of differences between supervisors at any level beyond the early stages of counsellor training. While he found that there were differences in levels of skilfulness across supervisors, there was little indication that supervisors improved with experience. He suggested that, although supervisors may not improve, they may change in what they offer to supervisees. For example, a new supervisor might promote identification between supervisee and supervisor, or have greater awareness of the issues facing trainees or demonstrate more enthusiasm. An experienced supervisor, on the other hand, might have greater technical skill, for example, in client assessment or in counselling interventions. Worthington (1987) cites a lack of training in supervision as a possible reason for the lack of improvement with experience and advocates supervision of supervision itself as a possible remedy.

As the experience of supervising grows, the supervisor develops an awareness of the demands of the role, of the aspects of it which are challenging as well as those in which the supervisor feels adequately skilled. Alonso (1983) has proposed a series of developmental milestones which can be applied to supervisors as they move from the position of novice supervisor to mid-career and then to late career stages. She describes the achievement of developmental tasks in three different areas, the first being the development of a sense of self as a supervisor, at the early stages of which the supervisor struggles with anxiety about the need for validation, for approval and for role models. The second section deals with what the supervisor brings to and takes from the supervisory relationship. The new supervisor may resemble an older sibling in the eyes of the supervisee – 'one who can still clearly remember what it feels like to be in the therapist's place, but for whom the competitive issues are still hot, while the intimacy issues reside primarily outside the relationship' (Alonso 1983: 31). The third area concerns the position of supervisors in relation to the institutional and administrative structure within which they work. She suggests that the young supervisor may need to be recognized by the institution as a non-student and therefore be unduly critical and rigorous towards the supervisee. Alternatively, the new supervisor may become over-identified with the supervisee because of unrepaired injuries left over from personal experience as a trainee.

A different model of supervisor development is proposed by Hess (1986, 1987). In this model, a beginning stage is characterized by the difficulty of role-status change and a focus more on the client than the counsellor and on techniques that will produce client change. An exploration stage follows in which the supervisor begins to identify with the role of supervisor and becomes more knowledgeable regarding supervision dynamics. Finally, a confirmation of supervisor-identity stage occurs, in which the central focus is on the supervisee's learning agenda (Bernard and Goodyear 1992). Supervisors can use their own supervision to reflect on how they are managing the new role, which parts of it they feel less confident about and whether they can identify any such stages in their work.

Preparation for supervision

As a therapist contemplates beginning to supervise, it will become apparent that certain issues need consideration which either do not arise in therapy or which require a different response.

Boundaries of supervision

The boundaries of the relationship between supervisor and supervisee are different in some respects from the boundaries between therapist and client. A therapist who is about to begin supervision can consider the differences in boundaries, particularly in relation to whom to supervise, confidentiality, limits of responsibility and accountability and the boundary between supervision and therapy.

- *Acquaintance* Supervisors and supervisees may know one another through working in the same setting or via other work-related contact. They may have other roles in relation to one another. This is different from the anonymity which is customary in the therapy relationship. The extent of the acquaintance and ongoing contact which is compatible with a supervisory relationship depends on the needs and level of experience of the supervisee and what is comfortable and manageable for both supervisor and supervisee. This is an issue which the supervisor and supervisee can look at together, considering how the pre-existing relationship and the supervisory relationship might affect one another, how to maintain the boundaries between these relationships and then deciding whether to undertake supervision or not. A related issue concerns the development of a supervisory relationship within a work setting and how attitudes of colleagues of the supervisor and supervisee may change.

- *Confidentiality* The boundaries surrounding confidentiality in supervision are similar to the boundaries of therapy, but there are some differences, for example, when supervision takes place on a training course and the supervisor has to write a report about the supervisee's development. When supervision is first set up, the supervisor and supervisee can discuss confidentiality, so that there is agreement about whom the supervisor might talk to and under what circumstances. Clear guidelines about confidentiality in supervision are offered in the British Association for Counselling Code of Ethics and Practice for the Supervision of Counsellors (1988).
- *Availability* Another boundary which may differ in supervision is the supervisor's availability outside sessions. A new supervisor can consider whether or how to be available outside supervision sessions for consultation when the supervisee is dealing with a crisis in therapy or needs to communicate urgently for some other reason.
- *Boundary between supervision and therapy* It is important for the supervisor to be clear about the boundary between supervision and therapy. There may be pressure to be the supervisee's therapist at times, which may appeal to the therapist and voyeur in the supervisor. This can arise as a result of a personal crisis in the supervisee's life or because of the supervisee's countertransference to a client or because of a supervisee's anxieties about being a therapist or being in supervision. Different models of supervision advocate different boundaries in these situations (see Chapter 2). It is usual, however, to address these feelings only in terms of how they impinge on the supervisee's therapeutic work while recommending that further exploration takes place within the supervisee's own therapy.
- *Accountability* The issue of accountability in supervision also requires attention when a therapist starts to undertake supervision and each time the supervisor takes on a supervisee in a new context. The new supervisor needs to be aware of the clinical and legal responsibility entailed in the role and of how these responsibilities may vary according to the context of the therapy which is being supervised. Bond (1993) suggests a framework for dividing the tasks of supervision and management which can help the therapist in clarifying the lines of accountability at the outset of supervision.
- *Evaluation* Unlike the therapist, the supervisor has the task of evaluating the work of the supervisee. Depending on the context of the supervision,

the function of evaluation varies. Supervision as part of a training course, for example, often contributes a key element in the overall evaluation of a student. However, evaluation may be less formal and may take the form of periodic reviews in ongoing supervision, in which both supervisor and supervisee reflect on the development of the supervisee's work, give feedback about the working of the supervisory relationship and discuss the use of future supervision. At the beginning of a new supervisory relationship, it can be useful to plan a review after a fixed number of sessions, so that doubts and concerns of either party can be aired. Bernard and Goodyear (1992) suggest various ways of making evaluation a more positive experience, advocating, for example, that evaluation procedures are spelt out in advance and that evaluation should be a mutual and continuous process.

The supervisee

When a supervisor takes on a supervisee for the first time, it is worth asking about the supervisee's therapeutic orientation, level of experience and supervision needs. In some situations the supervisor may have little choice about whether or not to see particular therapists for supervision. Clarification at this stage can influence such a decision and it can inform the supervisor's decision about how to supervise.

Therapeutic orientation of the supervisee

If the supervisor and supervisee share the same therapeutic orientation, supervision is likely to be easier for the supervisor and more satisfactory for the supervisee. Where the therapeutic orientation is different, there may be limitations to the supervision. For example, different therapeutic orientations advocate widely differing ways of understanding and working with a client's anxiety. If the supervisor and supervisee disagree about this issue, the supervisor might feel concerned and the supervisee might feel unsupported. If the differences are too fundamental, the supervisor may decide not to undertake supervision or to do so for a trial period, which can be reviewed.

However, a supervisee may approach a supervisor who uses a different therapeutic orientation, aware of this and with the purpose of learning from the supervisor's therapeutic perspective. In such a case, supervision can be profitable, though it is useful to be explicit about the differences in orientation and their implications for therapy. Where supervisors and supervisees share a therapeutic orientation, supervisees will develop their own style of doing therapy. Supervisors need to be tolerant and accepting of the supervisee's approach, and to offer but not impose their own.

Level of experience of the supervisee

Knowledge of the level of experience of a supervisee can influence the decision about whether or not to undertake supervision and, if the decision is made to offer supervision, this information can enable the supervisor to offer help appropriate to the supervisee's skills and needs. The various developmental models of supervision can aid the supervisor who is assessing the level of development of the supervisee and deciding on an appropriate approach in supervision. Littrell *et al.* (1979), Loganbill *et al.* (1982), Stoltenberg and Delworth (1987) and Hawkins and Shohet (1989) all propose such models, and reviews of developmental models, have been carried out by Holloway (1987) and Worthington (1987). These models describe the stages of development of counsellors and therapists, citing characteristics of therapists at different levels of development, a range of dimensions on which they may vary and their attitudes towards supervision and the supervisor at these different stages. The developmental models are useful in suggesting the different types of role that a supervisor may adopt according to the identified stage of development of the supervisee. Casement (1985: 32) describes the changing function of supervision as a trainee develops, proposing that the therapist needs to develop an 'internal supervisor' during the course of training and beyond and, as this grows, 'supervision should develop into a dialogue between the external supervisor and the internal supervisor'.

There are sometimes situations where a supervisor takes on for supervision a therapist who has more experience or higher qualifications. While this can prove productive and satisfactory, it can result in the supervisor, at least initially, deluging the supervisee with helpful comments in a bid to demonstrate superiority. Inexperienced supervisors must be clear about the limitations of their own competence as well as their expertise. In considering their own level of experience compared to that of the prospective supervisee, supervisors may decide that it would be in the best interests of the therapist not to enter into a supervisory relationship with them at this stage.

Style of supervision

It is useful for new supervisors to consider the style of supervision which they adopt, to be clear about their own natural tendencies and to be aware of the strengths and limitations of their own style. Styczynski (1980) asserts that style is often chosen unconsciously and limited by the supervisor's own way of relating to people. The new supervisor's choice of style is also likely to be affected by previous experience of supervision as a supervisee. Style can vary and may be didactic, supportive, therapeutic, theoretical, intellectual, confronting or reflective (Styczynski 1980).

Similarly, supervisors are likely to pay more attention to some aspects of therapy than others. Langs comments that:

every supervisor will have his preference for a particular communicative mode of his own, and will tend to focus his efforts on one of the three basic areas of unconscious communication between the patient and the therapist: the cognitive, the object relational, and the projective identificatory – the last two being essentially interactional (Langs, 1978). It is important for an unbiased experience that the supervisor be aware of his own propensities, and that he attempt to maintain a balanced approach to both the cognitive and interactional spheres in his supervisory work, despite the presence of biases. Similarly, he must be prepared equally to deal with frame issues, interactional problems, and essential intrapsychic contents within the patient, rather than tending to favor one or another particular focus.

(1980: 110)

Differences between supervisor and supervisee

Differences between supervisor and supervisee may extend beyond their therapeutic orientation and level of experience. They may differ in terms of their gender, sexual orientation, race, class, physical ability and age (see Chapter 11). A supervisor has a responsibility to be aware of how such differences might affect the expectations and experiences that the supervisor and supervisee have of one another. Such differences may also exist between the supervisee and the client, and supervision offers an opportunity to explore their impact on the therapy at both conscious and unconscious levels. In a chapter on supervision in a multi-cultural context, Bernard and Goodyear (1992: 222) state that they 'believe most minority issues can be diffused with time when openness is encouraged and there is good faith . . . in the therapy system it is the supervisor who has the most power to establish this kind of atmosphere . . . The largest task is to avoid making careless assumptions about others.'

This last point is underlined by research into the effects on the supervisory relationship of the level of experience and gender of the supervisor and supervisee, reported by Worthington and Stern (1985). They found that supervisees who had same-gender supervisors felt that they had closer relationships with them and that they were more influenced by them than supervisees who had other-gender supervisors. Ratings made by supervisors, however, indicated that they did not perceive the relationship in the same way as their supervisees; instead there were no significant differences between ratings of supervisors supervising same-gender supervisees and those supervising other-gender supervisees.

Use of supervision

When beginning a new supervisory relationship, the supervisor can suggest different ways of presenting work to the supervisee. These may include presenting one case in depth, focusing on technical or theoretical issues and using audiotapes (see Chapters 8 and 9) as well as the usual alternating presentation of several pieces of ongoing work. At different points in supervision it may be valuable to try to present work in different ways.

The relationship between the new supervisor and the supervisee

To practise supervision effectively, the supervisor has to be aware of the dynamics of the relationship, of the thoughts and feelings which the supervisor and supervisee may have about one another and of how these may help or hinder the process of supervision. A key issue for the new supervisor is that the role of supervisor confers authority on the therapist who assumes it. A supervisee invests the supervisor with power and authority and sees the supervisor as being in a position to judge. The supervision relationship may restimulate feelings in the supervisee which originate in previous relationships with authority, in particular parents (Hartung 1979). For a new supervisor who is inexperienced and perhaps unsure or anxious about the role, it may be difficult to accept and manage this aspect of it.

The supervisee may react to the authority of the supervisor's role in different ways, presenting feelings overtly or more indirectly. A supervisee may idealize and admire the supervisor; an inexperienced therapist may have a strong need to rely on the supervisor and therefore see them in this way. A new supervisor may be surprised at this or feel in need of praise and therefore feel gratified by the supervisee's attitude.

A supervisee may mistrust the perceived authority of the supervisor, anticipating criticism, censure or attempts to control. A supervisor's knowledge and perceptiveness may be frightening or intimidating to a supervisee (Langs 1980). These feelings can lead a supervisee to be guarded, to fear exposing mistakes or displaying vulnerability. Mistrust, shame and fear can make the supervisee withhold the very material which most needs attention in supervision. A supervisee may react to the supervisor's authority by taking control through asserting that the supervisor does not understand aspects of the supervisee's work and that the supervisee has superior knowledge. While there may be truth in this, it is communicated in a defensive way.

A supervisee may envy the supervisor's experience or knowledge or position and act this out by refusing to take in anything from the supervisor, dismissing what the supervisor says as worthless. If a supervisor can help the supervisee to acknowledge these feelings and reactions and look at how they are affecting the relationship, this can provide invaluable learning experience and at the same time free supervision to become a productive working alliance.

New supervisors bring to the role their own experiences and feelings regarding authority. Whether these originate from being in positions of authority or from relating to people in authority, they can have a significant effect on the relationship and on the course of supervision. There are two main ways, in which a new supervisor can approach the issue of authority, which are likely to constrain the process of supervision: denial of authority and over-identification with the authoritarian role.

A supervisor who denies the authority of the role may identify too closely with the supervisee. Identification can play an important part in supervision, but a supervisor who identifies too closely with the supervisee may not use understanding and insight that can be gained from having some distance and separateness. A new supervisor may want to be popular and well-liked (Styczynski 1980) and so relate in an over-friendly way, revealing large amounts of personal information. While this may relieve some of the supervisee's persecutory anxieties, it may also encroach on the space that a supervisee needs to explore and to be honest about themselves, their work and the supervision.

A new supervisor who denies the authority of the role may be too permissive and so, for example, would not be clear and firm in a situation where it is apparent that the supervisee is practising unethically or inappropriately. Such a supervisor might be overly supportive and might not challenge or confront issues which the supervisor knows may cause the supervisee anxiety and yet need to be faced (Styczynski 1980).

A new supervisor may, alternatively, react to the new role by embracing its authoritarian potential too readily. The supervisor then defends against the fear of not knowing by assuming a position which is authoritarian. This then leads the supervisor to be rigid and inflexible and, when challenging the supervisee, to be experienced as threatening and oppressive. The supervisor may not acknowledge what the supervisee can teach the supervisor and may not allow the supervisee to be right or to know better, although, of course, the supervisee does know the client better and, indeed, may be better at some aspects of therapy than the supervisor. The supervisor may adopt a smart, clever, omnipotent stance, being wise after the event, knowing the answers. Casement (1985: 24) describes the danger of offering too strong a model in supervision: 'this can mislead students into learning by a false process, borrowing too directly from a supervisor's way of working rather than developing their own. Some students can be seriously undermined in this way, feeling as if the treatment (or even the patient) has been taken over by the supervisor.'

New supervisors who assume too much authority in the role may establish too much distance between themselves and their supervisees. This can lead supervisees to feel that they are not adequately understood, supported or encouraged. Such supervisors may be unable to acknowledge their own mistakes and the contribution of these to difficulties in supervision, which can make supervisees feel confused and frustrated. They may indoctrinate supervisees, imposing their own style and approach, implicitly devaluing the supervisees'.

When supervisors demonstrate what they know and tell supervisees what they should do or should have done, rather than helping supervisees to explore what they do not know and find out for themselves what they need to know, they deprive the supervisees of an important learning experience. Searles writes that:

> One of my most oft-repeated experiences is that when I point out to the student how he should have responded, without helping him to discover what factors in the patient's psychopathology made it difficult for him so to respond, I do not actually help him; rather, I only leave him feeling more wrong, stupid and inadequate than ever.
>
> (1965: 589)

For new supervisors there may be an anxiety about knowing or knowing enough and a consequent fear of being found out by the supervisee. This can lead to a need to prove, both to themselves and to their supervisees, that they know, that they are competent. When supervisors deal with the pressure of this anxiety by demonstrating their knowledge, they are likely not only to undermine the supervisee but also to prevent the creation of an important place in supervision, a place where it is all right not to know. Both supervisee and supervisor need to feel that they can occupy this place. Paradoxically, it is from this place that deep understanding and fresh insight can come, which, in turn, help the supervisor and supervisee to know.

Conclusion

Becoming a supervisor is a process which requires careful consideration and preparation, but which can bring great rewards. Bernard and Goodyear (1992: 142) comment on the benefits and dangers of supervising:

> There are times when we can appreciate how far we have come by observing the tentative work of those under our charge ... There is something very self-assuring about having some experience and being able to see from where one has come. There also is something seductive, and even dangerous, about being in such a position: supervisors can forget to question their own competence.

Casement (1985: 33) describes the 'endless opportunities for therapists to re-examine their own work, when looking closely at the work of the person being supervised' and sees doing supervision as an opportunity to 'enter into a further phase of growth that recapitulates much of what has gone before'. Langs (1980:123) comments on the lack of reference to the gratification of supervisory work and asserts that supervisors have 'special opportunity for creativity and growth' because of the added distance between supervisor and client and because of the supervisor's different responsibilities.

For a therapist who is becoming a supervisor there is much to learn and much to look forward to. Perhaps a way to approach the challenges of supervision, and to guard against the dangers, is to think in terms of being in a continuous state of becoming, as Bion suggested (Bion 1975: 26, in Casement, 1985). Thus, becoming a supervisor is a process which begins when the therapist first contemplates undertaking the work and continues through taking on the first supervisees and beyond as the supervisor gains experience and develops within the role.

References

Alonso, A. (1983) A developmental theory of psychodynamic supervision. *The Clinical Supervisor,* 1(3): 23–36.
Bernard, J.M. and Goodyear, R.K. (1992) *Fundamentals of Clinical Supervision.* Boston, MA: Allyn and Bacon.
Bion, W.R. (1975) *Brazilian Lectures 2.* Rio de Janeiro: Imago Editora.
Bond, T. (1993) *Standards and Ethics for Counselling in Action.* London: Sage.
British Association for Counselling (1988) *Code of Ethics and Practice for the Supervision of Counsellors.* Rugby: BAC.
Casement, P. (1985) *On Learning from the Patient.* London: Routledge.
Hartung, B. (1979) The capacity to enter latency in learning pastoral psychotherapy. *Journal of Supervision and Training in Ministry,* 2: 46–59.
Hawkins, P. and Shohet, R. (1989) *Supervision in the Helping Professions.* Milton Keynes: Open University Press.
Hess, A.K. (1986) Growth in supervision. Stages of supervisee and supervisor development. *The Clinical Supervisor,* 4: 51–67.
Hess, A.K. (1987) Psychotherapy supervision. Stages, Buber, and a theory of relationship. *Professional Psychology: Research and Practice,* 18: 251–9.
Holloway, E.L. (1987) Developmental models of supervision. Is it supervision? *Professional Psychology: Research and Practice,* 18: 209–16.
Langs, R. (1978) *The Listening Process.* New York: Aronson.
Langs, R. (1980) Supervision and the bipersonal field, in A.K. Hess (ed.) *Psychotherapy Supervision: Theory, research and practice.* New York: John Wiley and Sons, Inc.
Littrell, J.M., Lee-Borden, N. and Lorenz, J.A. (1979) A developmental framework for counseling supervision. *Counselor Education and Supervision,* 19: 119–36.
Loganbill, C., Hardy, E. and Delworth, U. (1982) Supervision. A conceptual model. *The Counselling Psychologist* 10(1): 3–42.
Mander, G. (1993) Dyads and triads. Some thoughts on the nature of therapy supervision. *Journal of the Institute of Psychotherapy and Counselling,* 1: 1–10.
Searles, H. (1965) Problems of psychoanalytic supervision, in H. Searles, *Collected Papers on Schizophrenia and Related Subjects.* London: Hogarth.
Stoltenberg, C.D. and Delworth, U. (1987) *Supervising Counselors and Therapists: A developmental approach.* San Francisco: Jossey-Bass.
Styczynski, L.E. (1980) The transition from supervisee to supervisor, in A.K. Hess (ed.) *Psychotherapy Supervision: Theory, research and practice.* New York: John Wiley and Sons, Inc.
Worthington, E.L. (1987) Changes in supervision as counselors and supervisors gain experience. A review. *Professional Psychology: Research and Practice,* 18: 189–208.
Worthington, E.L. and Stern, A. (1985) Effects of supervisor and supervisee degree level and gender on the supervisory relationship. *Journal of Counselling Psychology,* 32(2): 252–62.

13

THE PLACE OF SUPERVISION

Geraldine Shipton

> When I came to Dungeness in the mid-eighties, I had no thought of building a garden. It looked impossible: shingle with no soil supported a sparse vegetation. Outside the front door a bed had been built – a rockery of broken bricks and concrete: it fitted in well. One day, walking on the beach at low tide, I noticed a magnificent flint. I brought it back and pulled out one of the bricks. Soon I had replaced all the rubble with flints. They were hard to find but after a storm a few more would appear. The bed looked great, like dragon's teeth – white and grey. My journey to the sea each morning had purpose.
>
> I decided to stop there: after all, the bleakness of Prospect Cottage was what had made me fall in love with it. At the back I planted a dog rose. Then I found a curious piece of driftwood and used this, and one of the necklaces of holey stones that I hung on the wall, to stake the rose. The garden had begun.
>
> (Jarman 1995: 12)

Derek Jarman's description of how he made a garden in the shingly wilds of Dungeness during the last years of his life, when he was dying of AIDS, is a memorable account of how a man uses limited time and space to produce an abundance of life and liveliness. In his garden are juxtaposed found objects; carefully planted, old, rusty gardening tools; standing stones; flowers; scented shrubs, sea kales; herbs and vegetables. His garden is not neat or conventional but 'shaggy' and surprising, some might say bizarre. Jarman's garden contains many of the same opposed categories which psychotherapy holds together: the planned and the accidental; the cultivated and the wild; the found and the made. Psychotherapy is like a garden in other respects too, taking place in the 'other' space of the consulting room, like a heterotopia as described by Foucault when he writes:

> There are also, probably in every culture, in every civilization, real places – places that do exist and that are formed in the very founding of society – which are something like counter-sites, a kind of effectively enacted utopia in which the real sites, all the other real sites that can be found within the culture, are simultaneously represented, contested, and inverted. Places of this kind are outside of all places, even though it may be possible to indicate their location in reality. Because these places are absolutely different from all the sites they reflect and speak about, I shall call them, by way of contrast to utopias, heterotopias.
>
> (1986: 24)

Foucault makes the garden explicitly heterotopic when he goes on:

> The traditional garden of the Persians was a sacred space that was supposed to bring together inside its rectangle four parts representing the four parts of the world, with a space still more sacred than the others that were like an umbilicus, the navel of the world at its centre (the basin and water-fountain were there); and all the vegetation of the garden was supposed to come together in the space, in this sort of microcosm ... The garden is the smallest parcel of the world and then it is the totality of the world. The garden has been a sort of happy, universalizing heterotopia since the beginnings of antiquity.
>
> (1986: 25–6)

The supervision of psychotherapy mirrors the array of odd juxtapositions in psychotherapy as the chapters of this book testify, and which this final chapter reiterates as it considers some very practical questions alongside more speculative ones. Supervision occupies a different space from therapy but it cannot be understood without being contrasted to it. Placing supervision between the two categories of training and therapy is unavoidable. In order to carry out these tasks I will look at the place of supervision, as a relationship which uses the insights developed in personal therapy and in training or education, without dissolving into either, and as evoked metaphorically as a place or image in the chapters of this book. This concluding chapter serves two functions: it brings the book to a close and it points to the future and the possibilities which have not been adequately dealt with in this book and which remain suspended in the air as questions.

Place

The idea of place has been evoked in many of the preceding chapters and it is to this metaphor that I now wish to turn. If psychotherapy is like a garden or a dream and takes place somewhere other than in day-to-day reality, where is supervision placed: in a public or private space? This question beats a rhythm throughout the book. A supervisor brings the professional networks of psychotherapy to the therapeutic dyad and interrupts the intimacy of patient and therapist, although some privacy is guaranteed for both, unless the supervisee commits a grave mistake, when supervision may become a place of inspection.

Various notions of looking are continuously evoked whenever supervision is being discussed, whether it is 'insight', 'inspection', 'speculation' or 'respect'. Hillman reminds us that:

> To look again is to 're-spect'. Each time we look at the same thing again, we gain respect for it and add respect to it, curiously discovering the innate relation of 'looks' – of regarding and being regarded, words in English that refer to dignity.
>
> (1989: 72)

The tensions between a predatory gaze and a respectful regard enter into the supervisory relation in this book; the former clearly setting up a series of defences against seeing and understanding, as Alan Lidmila, Peter Clarke and Jonathan Bradley discuss in their different ways. Respectful regard, on the other hand, creates an optimal climate for thinking about, and learning from experience.

Bureau

As well as a semi-private space, supervision is also an educational or bureaucratic space, successful traversal of which will ensure the award of a qualification to practice for trainees. David Edwards is keen to keep in sight the history of supervision's relation to training and to remind us of how 'the norm' or tradition has become established. Colin Lago and Joyce Thompson are concerned that what has become woven into 'normal' practice is a lack of awareness and sensitivity to racial and cultural difference and, even, an invitation to interact at one remove through a false identity.

However, for the supervisor, there is also a conspicuous lack of any kind of ritual which marks the coming of age. The passage from therapist to supervisor happens, at the moment, with no rite or acknowledgement, and furthermore with very little validation. How strange when this activity involves so many difficult and consequential considerations.

Microcosm

Supervision could be a microcosmic space where matters which are unregulated may also determine therapeutic work with patients: issues of discrimination or lack of recognition and respect for difference may be reproduced or amplified. This may be a matter of cultural or racial difference as mentioned above or, as Deborah Pickvance suggests, there might also be a difference centred on lack of awareness of the role of gender in supervisory relations. The supervisory relationship can then be seen as a crucible in which impurities are melded into the very fabric of therapeutic practice. This need not only mean that the 'product' is contaminated, as Langs (1994) suggests, when boundaries are violated, but that the result is stronger and more pliable if 'utopian' supervision can be tempered by some recognition of the day-to-day realities within which we all work. This applies also to Jim Gomersall's thoughts on how supervision can be provided or augmented in the National Health Service.

Archive

In this book supervision has also been likened to a kind of archive, a memory-bank where thoughts and responses can be accessed: Peter Clarke suggests IPR can facilitate such a process for supervisees. Similarly, Mark Aveline suggests that it is by means of a record of what has happened in therapy that supervisees can often learn from experience rather than simply repeat it. As David Edwards demonstrates, the practice of supervision is also a repository where the evolution of psychoanalytic traditions across history and geography is to be found.

Workspace

Supervision is, however, a place so full of possible interpretations and anxieties that in order for it to become a place of work, a space has to be cleared for thought. This is what Phil Mollon clarifies, although in a style that focuses less on the concrete aspects of making a good structure in which to root supervision, as Langs would argue, than on the subtle use of the supervisor's personal skill in containing and processing their own thoughts and feelings and the responses evoked by the supervisee. The *raison d'être* of this whole book is to acknowledge that we do not know all that there is to know about supervision but that it is an activity that takes place in a mental and emotional space that a good supervisor constructs afresh each time with the supervisee.

Both David Maclagan and John Henzell evoke the notion of an art space too, where the work of therapy can also be supported by the image and by fantasy in supervision. Jim Gomersall's use of a mandala echoes a related but essentially quite different concern for a pattern and container of the material of supervision. Phil Mollon, on the other hand, reminds us of the power of food metaphors when he makes an analogy between the raw and cooked and how a process changes what is raw and indigestible to something more humanized and usable, evoking not so much the modern kitchen, but the ancient homefires.

Superimposed spaces: therapy and supervision

The diversity of thinking and practice expressed in the chapters of this book mirror the complexity of supervision. However, they also belie the lack of adequate theorization of its foundations as one of the main influences on how psychotherapy is carried out and trainees develop their clinical skills. The other dominant mode of transmission of psychotherapy is personal therapy, which, in contrast, is highly theorized. In some respects, it is improper to disentangle the two concepts from each other as they form a therapeutic whole: supervision helps both the psychotherapist and the patient, suggesting a therapeutic regulation of therapy, while the unconscious of the patient may also exercise a supervisory effect on the therapist (Searles 1979) and 'speaks' to the supervisor, as Jonathan Bradley points out.

Different practices

Supervision differs from therapy in several ways, particularly in being subjected to some quite divergent practices. The ethical guidelines in supervision are much weaker than in psychotherapy, for example, and are only just becoming codified. Langs goes as far as suggesting that deviations from a solid frame around the boundaries of supervision result in direct and deleterious effects on both supervisee and patient. However, Langs's strong emphasis on the role of the frame, and on the decoding of repressed triggers which are activated by supervisors who fail to provide a safe, consistent frame, is extreme. His notion of the essential ground rules or *fixed frame of supervision* includes a setting which should be a professional workspace such as an office or consulting room, not a room in a domestic setting. It should be private, soundproofed and be the location of supervision for the entire duration of the supervisor–supervisee relationship. There should also be an agreed, fixed time for supervision which should not vary in frequency or length. Fees must be paid in a consistent manner and contractual arrangements adhered to meticulously by both partners in supervision, while self-disclosure and encounters outside of supervision should be avoided.

None of these aspects of securing a solid basis on which to work together is especially contentious in itself. However, the extent to which Langs sees deviations or contaminations of the supervisory set-up as potentially so destructive is controversial. He writes:

> Without exception, frame-securing interventions are derivatively confirmed by patients (and supervisees when the responsive narrative material is available): they do so via displaced and disguised, encoded stories of safe and creative spaces, well-functioning individuals, and the like. In contrast, frame alterations evoke non-confirmatory images of unsafe places, ignorance, assault, seduction, exploitation, and such.
>
> (1994: 60–1)

This is a radical view of the effects of the supervisor's behaviour on the patient's narrative and highlights the need for ethical rules of conduct and practice to be elaborated and debated. The suggestions made by Mark Aveline about occasional sharing of a supervisor's audio or videotape, for example, which could reduce the supervisee's anxiety and over-dependence on the authority and expertise of the supervisor, would be seen as a frame-deviant intervention by Langs. Evidence of 'frame-rupture' in the supervisee's account of the case-material would be anticipated by Langs, who would expect a harmful effect on the supervisor's capacity to work effectively. By putting one idea about good practice against another we can set up a more critical debate and questions can be formulated for research and discussion.

Time

Another difference between supervision and psychotherapy is that supervisors will relate to time-limited supervision in an altogether different manner than time-limited therapy. There is an expectation that the specific supervisory dyad will be terminable in practice, despite the need for supervision being interminable in principle, since ongoing supervision is a professional requirement in the codes of ethics of several accrediting bodies (e.g. BAC). A supervisee will often experience various supervisions during their training and after. This may not be as significant in schools of psychotherapy where a similar model of supervision is almost always followed (as in the focus on the delivery of case-material in sequential, almost verbatim format) but it makes an especially big impact on supervisees who may have to receive supervision from a person who uses a method of supervision which is new to the supervisee. In all cases, however, the personality of the supervisor will also be a significant factor in supervision. Recently, a very experienced supervisee asked why supervision should involve a close account of the session she had conducted with her client when this was not how she had previously understood the appropriate remit of supervision: she was afraid she would feel deskilled and wondered why this laborious convention was considered to be so important. She asked for some references so that she could read up about it.

Perhaps several of the chapters in this book go some way towards elucidating the rationale behind particular models of supervision, but arguments about the optimal method are few and far between. The supervisee's question can be understood on several levels but the point it raises which is pertinent here is that there is a lack of published debate about methods of supervision. Another moot point is whether or not a specific theoretical orientation can be taught 'through the back door' by taking people into supervision who have been trained in a different model. Is it a creative mix that is so concocted or an eclectic mess?

Rhythmicity

On the other hand, one of the similarities of supervision and psychotherapy is their rhythmicity. Deborah Pickvance mentions object-hunger as a professional hazard which supervision may alleviate: it may be that the companionship which supervision may offer is also linked to the rhythmic structuring of the working week. The emotional content of therapy is not predictable but supervision is more so and happens in a planned, regular way. Psychotherapy has the same external structure, but internal to a session is a dynamic that can be guessed at yet which will almost always take the therapist by surprise when it unfolds. Nevertheless, there is a remembering, repeating and working through which constitutes an underlying pattern in psychotherapy and which shows through in supervision. The pattern is often hard for a therapist to see when all three actions may entail enactment as well as speech.

Indeed, in working with very disturbed parts of the mind, therapists' ability to see and connect up what is presented comes under attack. Supervision provides a link to a community of psychotherapists and counsellors who know about these or similar experiences. If psychoanalysis was placed up alongside government and education – for Freud the 'impossible professions', as Jonathan Bradley reminds us – supervision is surely the art of combining all three tasks in supervision.

Supervision also provides, especially for trainees or newly qualified therapists, a reference point, an anchor to a supervisor who, perhaps, embodies the ethical 'government' of psychotherapy and counselling. In this respect, the role of the supervisor is to stay constant though flexible in the supervisee's travels across a spectrum of feelings and thoughts with their clients, accommodating the interplay of ocnophilic and philobatic needs in the supervisee (that is, the preference for proximity to an object; and the preference for letting go and enjoying the spaces between objects), as Michael Balint describes (1959). Supervisees will feel drawn to different kinds of relationship to their work and to the supervisor depending, amongst other things, on their own negotiated relationship with time, distance and objects.

Research

It is obvious from the foregoing commentary that more research about supervision is needed and opportunities for developing the ability to help others perform their therapeutic work are desirable. The idea of training courses is not the only option, although these seem to be proliferating. Another approach would be Tavistock-style 'work discussion' groups chaired by very experienced supervisors where presentations of supervisory cases (with permission, of course, from supervisees), are discussed and commented on so that the supervision of supervision is developed and becomes a theorized and debated area.

As we move into a period of intense technological expansion where the concept of space and place are extended through 'cyberspace', it is interesting to think about what is contained within a supervisory 'secure frame'. We need to consider whether or not supervision over the telephone, teleconferencing, Internet supervision, Internet supervisory groups are all potential media for the development of supervision; or whether there is a real necessity to ensure that supervision is guaranteed its own time and place in the shared space of everyday routine rather than in virtual reality?

Finally, it is hard to draw together the chapters of a book which has evolved over several years rather than been planned from its inception. In trying to force some shape upon the text, I risk distorting what others have tried carefully to outline with precision. Despite this I will close by echoing a thought from the Introduction which is about the nature of curiosity and its cautious management in supervision. Outside supervision, that is, in the discussions within a book such as this, where we can generalize and exaggerate, curiosity can be a helpful partner in ensuring that the quality of supervision and psychotherapy is debated. I hope that this final part of the book has allowed curiosity to rule in a benign fashion, much as William James suggested, and that it has usefully followed his other recommendations when he wrote: 'First, I say, irrepressible curiosity imperiously leads one on; and I say that it always leads to a better understanding of a thing's significance to consider its exaggerations and perversions, its equivalence, and substitutes and nearest relatives everywhere' (1901: 21–2). The nearest relative of supervision is psychotherapy, and a substitute is the art of making a garden. Like Jarman, this means using practical skills, theory and imagination but it also means respecting what is there to be found.

References

Balint, M. (1959) *Thrills and Regressions*. New York: International Universities Press.
Foucault, M. (1986) Of other spaces. *Diacritics*, Spring: 22–7.
Hillman, J. (1989) From mirror to window. Curing psychoanalysis of its narcissism. *Spring*, 49: 62–75.
James, W. (1901) *The Varieties of Religious Experience*. Harmondsworth: Penguin, 1985.
Jarman, D. (1995) *Derek Jarman's Garden*. London: Thames and Hudson.
Langs, R. (1994) *Doing Supervision and Being Supervised*. London: Karnac.
Searles, H. (1979) *Countertransference and Related Subjects*. New York: International Universities Press.

INDEX

N.B. Bold numbers indicate a diagram

absent events, reports as, 71
'active' fantasy, 'passive' fantasy and, 64
Adam and Eve myth, shame and sin, 37
affect simulation, IPR and, 95
Allen, P., 95, 98, 102
Alonso, A., 132, 133, 134
Analysenkontrolle, 16, 20
analysts, defensive mechanisms and, 49
art therapists, 4, 5, 13, 19, 68, 73
    appropriate supervision and, 69
    National Health Service and, 20
art therapy, 67, 68, 71, 73
art-works, fantasy, 68
'artist fantasy', 63
Association of Black Counsellors (ABC), 119–20
Atkinson, D., 120, 122
audio or video equipment, 5, 19
audio- or videotapes
    IPR and, 94, 103
    privacy, confidentiality and ethical considerations, 81
    selective and sensitive use, 82, 91–2
    supervision and, 14, 19, 77, 80, 82
Aveline, M., 5, 14, 17, 83, 85, 100, 146

Balint, M., 17, 18, 111, 112, 113, 149
'bare attention', 39
Barthes, R., 37, 38, 40

Batten, C., 15, 121
Bernard, J.M., 14, 134, 136, 138, 141
Betcher, W.R., 15, 37
Bibring, E., 16, 17
Bion, W.R.D., 28, 47, 48, 142
Bollas, C., 2, 41
Bond, T., 15, 135
Bradley, J., 4, 51, 147, 149
British Association of Art Therapists (BAAT), 19
British Association for Counselling (BAC), 13, 14, 119, 129, 148
'bug in the ear', supervision and, 14
'burnout', 18

Casement, P., 16, 41, 137, 140, 141, 142
Champernowne, Gilbert and Irene, 73
Chandler, R., 40, 41
child psychotherapist, example of work, 53–4
childhood
    basis for knowledge, 35–6
    coercion of and recording, 83
    supervision and, 39
Clarke, P., 4, 5, 145, 146
'class structure' of fantasy, 64
client, factors which can illuminate or obscure, 52–3

client-supervisee *amour-fou*, supervisor and, 40
clinical psychologists, 13
communication
 client-therapist, **124**
 conversation, 74–5
 direct, **125**, **127**
 function of consciousness in, 27
 hemispheres of the brain and, 33
 IPR, 94, 100
 problem, 54
 projective identification and, 49
 proxy-self, 124, **125**
 significant when recorder is off, 87
 therapist and breakdown, 53, 55
 therapist and patient and, 47
'communitas', 36
competitiveness, effect on thinking space, 32
Conan Doyle, A., 41–2
confidentiality, consent to tape and, 81, 87, 89–90
consciousness
 fantasy and, 62
 function of, 27
contemporary society, cultural diversity and, 121
counsellors, 4, 6, 13, 18, 93
countertransference
 fantasy and, 66, 81
 group-based approach, 18
 the hunch or intuition and, 42
 psychotherapy and, 2–3, 49
 supervisee's problems and, 72
 taping patient and, 91
cross-cultural supervision, 5, 15
cross-orientation supervision, 6
cross-profession supervision, 6
curiosity and shame, knowledge and, 37–8
'cyberspace', 150

defensive diversions, IPR and, 95
defensive reaction, 'not knowing' and, 36, 39
defensive supervisee, what is not known, 38
'democratic' models of therapy, fantasy and, 65

developmental models, role of supervisor and, 137
diagrammatic images, embodied images and, 76
didactic model of supervision, 13, 16–17
'discovery learning', IPR and, 94, 98
'distance to the literal' in supervision, 4
Doehrman, M.J., 15, 80
Don Quixote, 35
'double matrix model' of supervision, 16
'dream reports', 71
dreaming, 28, 30, 63, 65

Eastern or Zen 'way of supervision', 38, 45
eclecticism, supervision and, 6, 72, 118
Eco, U., 41, 44
educational psychologists, 13
Edwards, D., 3, 4, 13, 145, 146
embodied images, diagrammatic images and, 76
'emotional storm', 47
'epistomphilic impulse', Klein and, 38
ethical issues, supervision and, 6, 15, 81, 89–90, 148
'evenly-suspended attention', 81, 84
experience, learning and, 25
experiental model of supervision, 16–17
'exploratory', 94
expressive play of children, free association of adults and, 50

'facilitative response modes', IPR and, 94
fantasy, 4, 7, 61–2, 81
 'class structure' of, 64
 dangers of, 68
 disqualification of, 63–5
 group, collective function of, 66–7
 in supervision, 67–8, 81
 towards a conscious approach to, 62–3, 68
 unconscious determination of, 61–2
 working with as an ally, 65–7
'fantasy blind', 62
fantasy, dreaming and aesthetic reaction, philosophy and psychology, 61
flexibility, supervisory relationship and, 12–13
forms of knowing, 35–7

Foucault, M., 143–4
Four-Countries Conference (1935), 16
'free association', 18, 24, 33, 39, 50, 62, 81
free-floating attention, 42
'freedom of expression', 2
Freud, S., 11, 69, 149
  analytic relationship, 48, 49
  concept of negation, 41
  countertransferences, 42
  fantasy, suspicion of, 61–2
  listening, 81
  psychotherapeutic relationships and, 11
  talking therapy, 71, 73, 74
  unconscious phantasy, 38, 63, 77

Geisteswissenschaften ('sciences of the spirit'), 73
general practitioners, 6, 18
'global workspace', 27
'go on observing', 47
Gomersall, J., 5, 6, 111
Goodyear, R.K., 134, 136, 138, 141
groups, supervisory space and, 32
Guggenbuhl-Craig, A., 67, 83
guilt
  communication breakdown, 53
  supervisee and, 43

Hawkins, P., 1, 2, 16, 137
Heart of Darkness, 35
Henzell, J., 5, 146
Hess, A.K., 14, 131, 133, 134
Hillman, J., 63, 65, 68, 73, 145, 160
Holloway, E.L., 12, 121, 137
'honest labelling', 94
'honesty time', 110
Howard, K., 108, 114
Hungarian school of psychoanalysis, 3, 16–17, 18

ignorance, shame and, 36
image, the, 5, 73–5
  embodiment and diagram, 75–6
  equality of looking together, 75
  psychotherapy and supervision, 72–3
  speech and aesthetics, 76–8
  in supervision, 71–2

'Imagery, raw and cooked. A hemispheric recipe', 33
individual recall, inquirer role and, 96–7
'ineffable', impact of an image, 76
inquirer
  ground rules for, 96–7, 99
  skill in selecting leads, 101
inquirer leads, examples, 96–7, 100
inquirer role, 93
  difficulties in enacting, 100–1
  individual recall and, 96–7
  IPR and, 93
  power in hands of recaller, 99
  supervisor in, 94
inquisitorial model of supervision, 43–4
insight, 47, 48–9, 50, 56, 68, 145
'inspection', 145
instructor's manual, IPR and, 93
'internal supervisor', 41, 94, 101, 137
International Psychoanalytical Association, 17
Internet supervisory groups, 150
'interpersonal allergies,' 95
Interpersonal Process Recall, *see* IPR
introjective identification, therapist and, 52
intrusiveness, shame and, 39
IPR, 4, 7, 93, 146
  compared with other psychotherapeutic traditions, 98–9
  in context of supervision, 94
  evaluation, 100
  exposition of the method, 94–5
  individual recall and inquirer role, 96–7
  mutual recall, 97–8
    issues about, 101–2
  resources needed, 102–3
  structure of training, 98

Jarman, D., 143, 150
Jung, C.G., 71, 74, 107
  fantasy and, 63–6, 68
  images and, 75, 77
  Tavistock lectures (1937), 64

Kagan, N., 19
  IPR and, 93–100, 102, 103
Kant, E., 74, 77

Karpman, S.B., **115–16**, 117
Klein, M., 38, 49–50, 53, 61, 73
knowledge
 curiosity and shame, 37–8
 forms of, 35–7, 44
 intrusion, secrecy and possession, 38–9
 oedipal triangle, 39
 supervisory pair and, 39–40
'knowledge by acquaintance', 4, 50, 51, 53, 55
'knowledge by description', 4, 50
Kontrollanalyse, 16, 20
Kovacs, V., 16, 17

Lacan, 73, 76
'lack of a sense of place', human unhappiness and, 108, 114
Lago, C.O., 5, 120, 145
Langs, R.
 books on supervision, 1–2
 supervision and, 146, 147
 supervisors and, 43, 132–3, 137–8, 139, 141, 148
latent meanings, fantasy and, 66
leaderless groups, disadvantages of, 109
learning, research and experience, 25
Lee, C.C., 120, 129
left hemisphere, information processing, 25
Lidmila, A., 4, 38, 145
Limited Consent Form, 89
'listening', 94
literature
 clinical supervision and, 1, 11, 12, 20, 73
 pairings and, 35
 on race and culture in therapy, 121
 studies institutions, 111
 on supervision, 1–2, 4
London Institute of Psycho-Analysis, 17

Maclagan, D., 4, 68–9, 146
mandala, peer group help using, 114–17, 146
Manufacturing, Science and Finance Trade Union (MSF), 19
Michigan State University, 93
micro-analysis, key moments and, 83, 85

migration patterns, cultural diversity and, 121
Moby Dick, 35
modes of enquiry in supervision, 35, 40
 the detective, 40–3
 the inquisitorial, 43–4
 the librarian, 44
Mollon, P., 4, 14, 17, 24, 39, 146
Money-Kyrle, R., 52, 53, 55
multi-disciplinary group of therapeutic helpers, peer group and, 107
multi-disciplinary supervision, issues of, 20

Name of the Rose, The, 41
National Health Service, 5, 18, 20
natural science, scientific enquiry and, 74
Naturwissenschaften (Natural science), 73–4
new supervisor, relationship with supervisee, 139–41
non-directed thinking, fantasy, 66
normal countertransference, therapist's attitude to patient and, 52
Nottingham Psychotherapy Training Courses, 85
nurses, 6

occupational therapists, 5, 19
oedipal triangle, supervisory pair and, 39–40
omissions, importance of, 81
one-way screen, supervision and, 14, 82, 87

'parental' knowledge, desired and feared, 38
'passive' fantasy, 'active' fantasy and, 64
patient
 acknowledging work of supervisee with, 31
 break-up, breakdown, breakthrough, 53–4
 factors which can illuminate or obscure, 52–3
 meaning of being taped, 87–8, 91
 normal or correct attitude to, 52
 pictorial work in psychotherapy, 73
 picture, therapist and supervisor, 78

process of supervision and, 47–8
supervision, struggle to keep in view, 50–2
Pedder, J., 12, 13, 17, 18
Pedersen, P.B., 120, 129
peer group supervision, 109
  clinical example using a mandala, 114–17
  for counselling and psychotherapy supervision, 110–11
  forms of, 110
  ground rules, 113
  growth of expertise in, 112
  interaction, 113–14
  need for, 107
  practical aspects of setting up, 111–12
  question of absent leader, 108–10
  size, admission and leaving, 112–13
  two principal tasks of, 108
  understanding organizations and, 117–18
  value of, 107–8, 118
persecutory experience
  inquisitorial mode of enquiry, 43
  process of knowing, 35, 37, 39
  of recording for patient, 87–8
  supervisee and, 43
  supervisor and, 68
Personal communication
  (1992), 98, 103
  (1995), 95, 98, 102, 104
'personal help', 111
'personal nightmares', 95
Peters, T., 111, 118
phantasy, 7, 35
  psychoanalytic understanding of, 62
  shaming, defensiveness and, 39
photographs, misleading representation, 71, 78
Pickvance, D., 5, 6, 145, 149
'picture puzzles', images of fantasy and, 75
place of supervision, 5, 143–4
  archive or memory bank, 146
  a bureaucratic space, 145
  and difference from therapy, 147–8
  time, 148
  metaphor of place and, 144–5
  microcosmic space, 145–6

rhythmicity and, 149
superimposed spaces in, 147
workspace, 146
pleasure principle, fantasy and, 61
post-Freudian therapists, 71, 73
preparation for supervision, 5, 134
  boundaries, 134
  accountability, 135
  acquaintance, 134–5
  availability, 135
  confidentiality, 135
  evaluation, 135–6
  supervision and therapy, 135
privacy, supervision and, 15, 37, 81, 84
process model, supervisors and, 1–2
professionals, active fantasy and, 64–5
projective identification, transference, countertransference and communication, 49
prospective analysts, rigorous training analysis, 49
'proxy-self', 124–5, 126, **127–8**
psychiatric nurses, 13, 18
psychiatrists, 19
psychoanalysis
  Britain and United States and, 74
  influence on supervision, 12
psychoanalysts, 18
psychoanalytical supervision, views of the patient, 48
psychologists, 6, 20
psychotherapeutic process, training and, 12
psychotherapeutic relationships, supervision and, 11
psychotherapists, 4, 13, 19, 93
  anal preoccupation with dirt, 42
  eclecticism and, 6
  emotional impact on, 18
  in talking therapy, 71
psychotherapy, 1–2
  actual visual images and, 74
  the image and, 73–5
  loneliness, 42
  'self-regulation' and, 19
  'sleuthing' mode of enquiry, 40
  supervision, 72–3, 150
  supervisor and, 1–2
psychotherapy courses, 17, 18, 85

psychotherapy supervision
  acquisitive approach and, 44
  process of discovery, 35
psychotic mind, experience and, 28

quasi-understanding, substitute for unknown truth, 28

'Race Awareness in Counselling Education' (RACE), 119, 129
race and culture in supervision, 5, 119–20, **123**, 145
real thinking, 28
'reality' factors, 2
recaller
  audio-recording and, 98
  relationship with inquirer, 99
  reponsibilities of, 96
recordings
  advantages and disadvantages, 82–5
  inquiry method and, 100
  making, 90–1
  psychoanalytic psychotherapists and, 80–1
  for therapist's benefit, 87
  using is controversial, 80–2
reflective thinking
  clues that indicate avoidance of, 30
  reverie and, 24
research, supervision and, 149–50
'respect', 145
reverie, reflective thinking and, 24
rhythmicity, supervision and psychotherapy, 149
right hemisphere, emotional information-processing and, 25
Rioch, M.J., 82, 86
'rivalry of naming', 40
Robinson Crusoe, 35
Rogers, C.R., 19, 122
Russell, Bertrand, 50

safety
  as container for supervisee, 30–1, 81
  knowledge and, 44
Saviour, role in peer group, **116**, 117
Schaverien, J., 75, 76
Searles, H.F., 15, 141, 147
security, tapes and, 85, 92

self-help organizations, peer group and, 108
selfobject functions, supervisor and, 28
shame
  Adam and Eve myth, 37
  dynamics in forms of enquiry, 43–4
  ignorance and, 36
  intrusiveness and, 39
shaming relation, unconscious phantasy and, 36–7, 39, 41
'Sheffield' model of supervision, 2–3
Sheffield, peer groups for GPs, 111, 113
Shohet, R., 1, 2, 16, 137
significant communications, recorder and, 87
silence, intolerance of, 30
'sleuthing' mode of enquiry, 40
'social dreaming matrix', 67
social workers, 6, 13, 18, 20
space for thinking
  functions of supervisor in building, 27–8
  groups and the supervisory, 32–3
  left- and right-brain, 24–5
    karate man, 26–7
    self-contained flat, 25–6
  'raw and cooked' emotional material, 33
  supervision as, 24
'speculation', 145
Styczynski, L.E., 133, 137, 140
supervisees
  ambivalent relationship to supervisor, 38
  defensive, 38
  desire to know, 38, 39, 45
  fantasy and, 67, 68
  guilt and, 43
  identity of, 5–7
  IPR and, 94
  level of experience of, 12, 137
  location of desire and, 39
  need to remain silent, 37
  phantasies of persecution and, 43
  privacy and, 84
  supervision and, 12
  techniques for right-brain mode of thinking, 31
  therapeutic orientation of, 136

supervision, 1, 13, 72, 109
  cardinal element in training, 80
  complexity, 7
    trans-cultural/trans-racial, 121–2, 129
  Eastern or Zen way, 38, 45
  eclecticism and, 6
  exploration and, 35, 44, 45
  fantasy in, 67–8
  framework for, 30–1, 147
  functions of, 12, 24
    in building the space, 27–8
  global workspace and, 27
  how it may be provided, 13–14
  image present in, 72, 76, 77
  influence of psychoanalysis, 12, 19
  IPR in the context of, 94
  issue of *therapeutic*, 17
  knowledge, complex dynamic relations, 40, 44
  need for multi-disciplinary training in, 20
  novel ideas about, 2
  oedipal configurations and, 40
  as process of waking up, 29
  project centred on knowing, 35
  psychoanalytic legacy, 17–19
  psychotherapeutic relationships and, 11
  psychotherapy and, 72–3
  race and culture, **123**
  research needed, 149–50
  sharing in fantasy and, 63
  space for thinking, 4, 24
  struggle to keep patient in view, 50–2
  therapy using images, 72
  two typical forms, 72–3
  use of tapes in, 85–6
supervision group, culture and personality of supervisor, 32
supervision and psychotherapy, rhythmicity and, 149
supervision of therapists, image-making clients and, 71
supervision today
  exposition of the didactic and experiential models, 16–17
  psychoanalytical legacy, 17–19

  some functions of a supervisor, 13–14
  tensions between training and developmental role of supervisor, 14–15
supervisors
  audio- or video recording and, 82
  client-supervisee *amour-fou* and, 40
  enquiry lines and, 31
  fantasy and, 66, 67, 68
  functions of, 13–14, 15
  hears patient and therapist, 27
  listening with *third ear*, 81
  'need to know' and, 37, 39
  needs of supervisee and, 12
  professional power of role, 121
  reasons for becoming, 131–2
  responsibility to patients, 43
  role, 47
    preparation and, 132–4
  selfobject functions and, 28
  state of mind of, 55
  style of supervision, 137–8
  supervisee, 136
    level of experience of, 137
    therapeutic orientation of, 13, 136
  systematic model for, 1
  tapes for supervision by supervisees, 86
  tensions between training and developmental role, 14–15
  use of supervision by, 138–9
supervisors of professionals, training supervisors and, 4
supervisors and trainees, effect of mismatch, 14, 19
supervisory dyad, problems with knowing, 37
supervisory effect on supervision, images and, 72
supervisory matrix, **120**
supervisory pair, oedipal triangle and, 39–40
supervisory relationship
  flexibility and, 12–13
  proxy-self idea and, **127**, **128**
  transference issues and, 15
supervisory space, groups and, 32
supervisory task, revelation of a third hidden part, 39–40

taping
  confidentiality and, 87
  consent elective, 89, 92
  patient's reactions, 5, 87–8
  selectively and sensitively used, 91–2
  supervisory aid, 84
  theoretical and practical
    disadvantages, 91
Tavistock Clinic (London), 18
Tavistock-style 'work discussion' groups,
  149
teleconferencing, 150
telephone supervision, 150
therapeutic relationship
  development of insight and, 6, 48
  video camera and, 20
therapeutic setting, use of fantasy, 67
therapist
  fantasy and, 66
  introjective identification with patient,
    52
  obscuring factors belonging to, 53
  personal therapy and, 17
  pictorial work in psychotherapy, 73
  taping and, 83
  transference love and, 42
therapist and patient
  countertransference phenomena and,
    52
  power differential, 89
  relationship and supervision, 47
  supervisor and, 47
therapist and supervisor, patient kept in
  view, 48
therapists and supervisors,
  psychodynamic implications for,
  48–50
therapy
  audio- or video recordings, 80
  creative use of fantasy and, 68
  difficulties in relationship, 56
  effect of recording on, 83
  image in, 77
  impact of race and culture upon,
    120–2
  painting, drawing or sculpture and, 71
  quality of pictures used in, 75–6
  structured within language, 77
  supervision, 147

different practices, 147–8
time and, 148
'there-and-then', 96, 102
thinking
  interferences with freedom of
    thought, 30–1
  thought police example, 31–2
  not thinking, dreaming and waking
    up, 28
  two robots example, 29–30
third ear, 81
Thompson, J., 5, 120, 122, 145
training, psychotherapeutic process and,
  12
training supervisions, supervisors of
  professionals and, 4
trans-cultural/trans-racial supervision
  complexity of, 121–2
  curved side, 122–6
  triangular relationship, 122
  with curved sides, 125–6, **128**
transference issues, supervisory
  relationship and, 15, 40, 49
transference phenomenon, images and,
  75

unconscious phantasy
  Klein's thinking and, 38
  nature of, 5, 7
  psychoanalytic view of fantasy and, 62
  shaming relation and, 39
the unconscious, 'inner speech acts', 77
United Kingdom Council for
  Psychotherapy, 14, 148
United States, 4, 121, 129
University of Houston, 93
'unveiling of the truth', narrative and,
  37

video camera, therapeutic relationship
  and, 20
videotape, supervisory session and, 86
Viennese school of psychoanalysis, 3,
  16–17

waking up, role of therapist in patient's
  dream, 30
Winnicott, D.W., 40, 73, 122
Wittgenstein, L., 74, 76

Woodmassey, A.C., 18, 19
word-play, fantasy and, 65–6
'working alliance' in psychotherapy, 6
Worthington, E.L., 133, 137, 138

Yalom, I.D., 108, 109

Zinberg, N.E., 15, 37

IN SEARCH OF SUPERVISION
Michael Jacobs (ed.)

Following the success of *In Search of a Therapist*, this final book in the series provides a unique window into the supervisory process. It takes a session, with background information, from the editor's own work with a long-term client, Ruth, and presents the dilemmas faced by the therapist to five supervisors – each one from very different therapeutic traditions:

- communicative psychotherapy
- self-psychology
- person-centered psychotherapy
- cognitive-behavioural therapy
- family therapy

In Search of Supervision offers the first real insight into the process of supervision of an actual session and enables counsellors and therapists to see how different orientations or schools of therapy and counselling react to and understand the same client and therapist. This fascinating book ends with a final chapter in which the therapist and client comment on the impact of the five supervisors on the work of their therapy together.

In Search of Supervision will be of interest to a wide range of counsellors and therapists, not only those working as or training as supervisors, but all those who experience supervision.

Contents
Michael Jacobs: in search of a supervisor – Ruth and Michael Jacobs: the session for supervision – The reader's response – Alan Cartwright: psychoanalytic self psychology – Prue Conradi: person-centered therapy – Melanie Fennell: cognitive-behaviour therapy – David Livingstone Smith: communicative psychotherapy – Sue Walrond-Skinner: family therapy – Michael Jacobs and Ruth: review and response.

Contributors
Alan Cartwright, Prue Conradi, Melanie Fennell, David Livingstone Smith, Sue Walrond-Skinner.

190pp   0 355 19258 0 (Paperback)

SUPERVISION IN THE HELPING PROFESSIONS
Peter Hawkins and Robin Shohet

Peter Hawkins and Robin Shohet explore the purposes and different forms of supervision and why it is crucial in the helping professions. They stress the need for commitment from both supervisor and supervisee alike, and provide guidelines and options for them both.

The book is divided into four parts. 'The supervisee's perspective' examines why we become helpers, and shows how we can be more effective in that role by ensuring we get the support and supervision we need. 'Becoming a supervisor and the process of supervision' discusses the transition from supervisee to supervisor, the various maps and models of supervision, and how supervisors should themselves be supervised, trained and developed. 'Group, team and peer group supervision' looks at other than one-to-one supervision, analyses the advantages and disadvantages of supervising in a group setting, and advises on how to manage group dynamics. 'An organizational approach' focuses on how to help an organization develop a learning culture where supervision is regarded as an intrinsic part of the work environment.

This is essential reading for counsellors, psychotherapists, social workers, probation officers, and all those in the helping professions.

> This book makes a significant contribution to the relatively sparse literature in the UK on supervision in the caring professions for the individual, the team and the organization. The authors present a new double matrix model of supervision which has been developed out of their own considerable practice experience. Its use is illustrated by numerous relevant examples and the generic principles underpinning their approach. New and experienced supervisors will find this a comprehensive and valuable book which will enrich their insights and their practice.
> Professor Ron Baker

Contents
Part 1: The supervisee's perspective – 'Good-enough' supervision – Why be a helper? – Getting the support and supervision you need – Part 2: Becoming a supervisor and the process of supervision – Becoming a supervisor – Maps and models of supervision – A process model of supervision – Supervisor training and development – Part 3: Group, team and peer-group supervision – Exploring the dynamics of groups, teams and peer groups – Part 4: An organizational approach – Supervising networks – Towards a learning culture – Bringing about change in teams and organizations – Conclusion: The wounded helper – Bibliography – Resources – Index.

176pp   0 335 09833 9 (Paperback)

THE SOCIAL WORK SUPERVISOR
SUPERVISION IN COMMUNITY, DAY CARE AND RESIDENTIAL SETTINGS

Allan Brown and Iain Bourne

The Social Work Supervisor is the first comprehensive British text on supervision of staff in social work, community care and social welfare settings. It examines the changing social work scene of the 1990s, and breaks new ground in areas such as:

- anti-oppressive supervision
- supervision of post-traumatic stress
- group supervision.

The Social Work Supervisor is a comprehensive text for the social work supervisor, and for all supervisors in social welfare and community care settings. It includes new material not found in other books on supervision. The authors emphasize the importance of the supervisory relationship, regular skilled supervision and a clear value base in the provision of good quality services.

This book provides a clear theoretical framework, bringing theory and practice together through numerous practical examples of supervision in action. One major chapter examines a range of typical supervision situations, and provides suggestions for possible supervisor responses.

The Social Work Supervisor will be invaluable reading for new and experienced supervisors; practice-teachers supervising students; trainers of supervisors; and social work managers.

Contents
Introduction – Setting the scene – The making of a supervisor – Supervision and power: an anti-oppressive perspective – Getting started: contracts and boundaries – A model for practice – The supervision relationship – Stress and trauma: the supervisor's response – Supervision and the team – Group supervision – Training and development – Core themes in a time of change – References – Index.

208pp   0 335 19458 3 (Paperback)   0 335 19459 1 (Hardback)